AF305162

ALINE DIÉPOIS & THOMAS GIZOLME

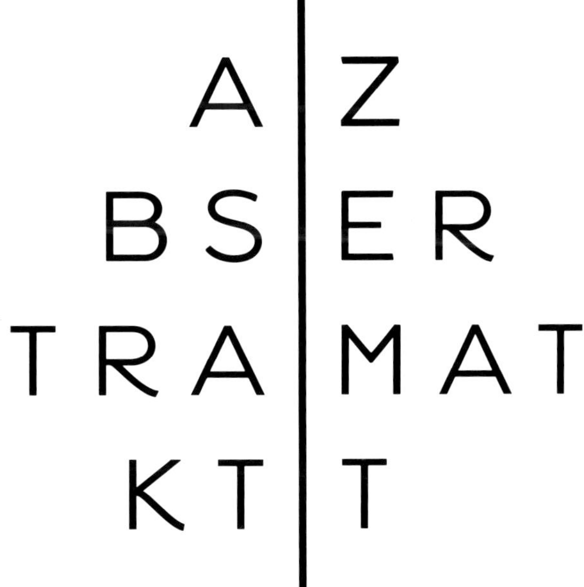

STEIDL

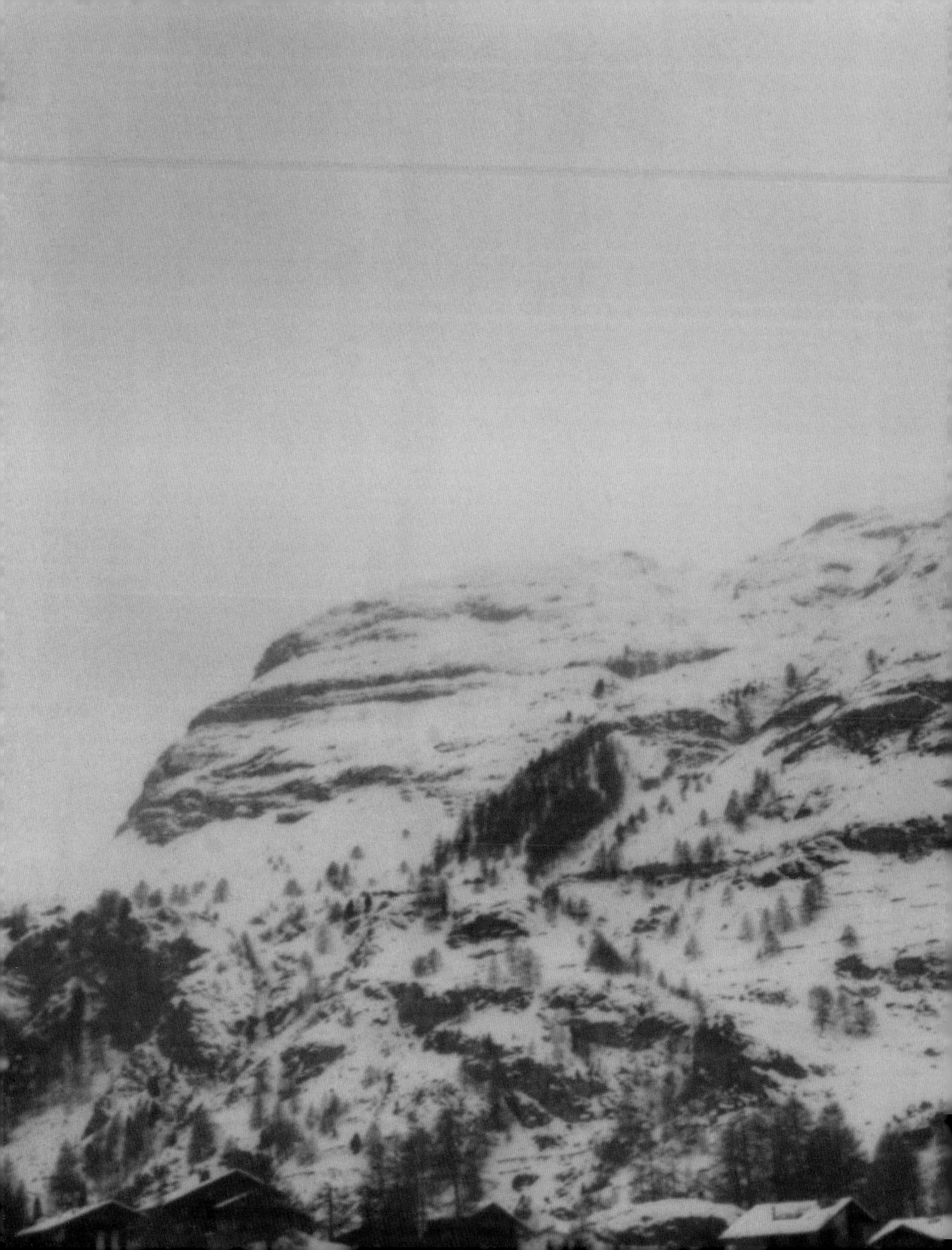

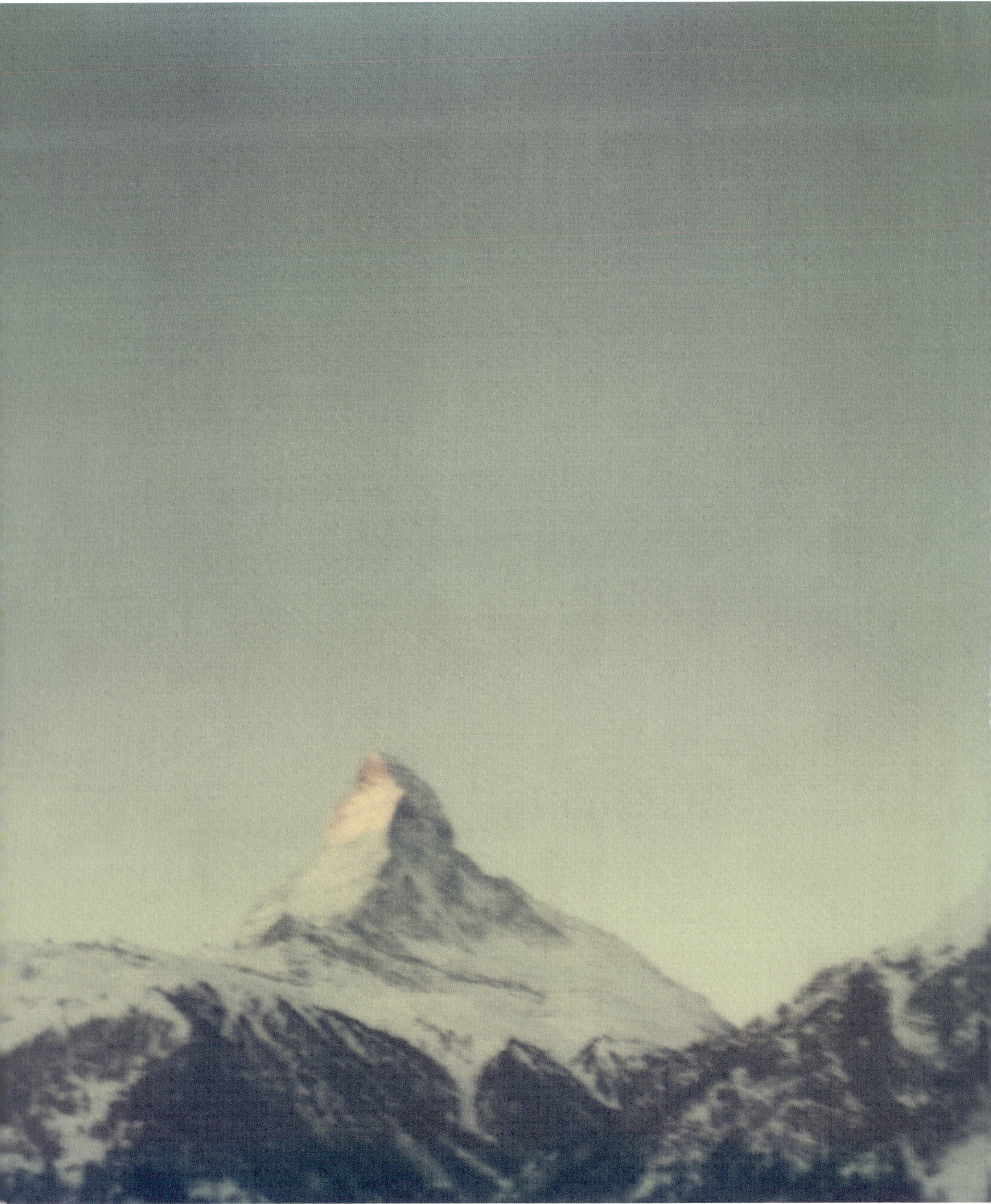

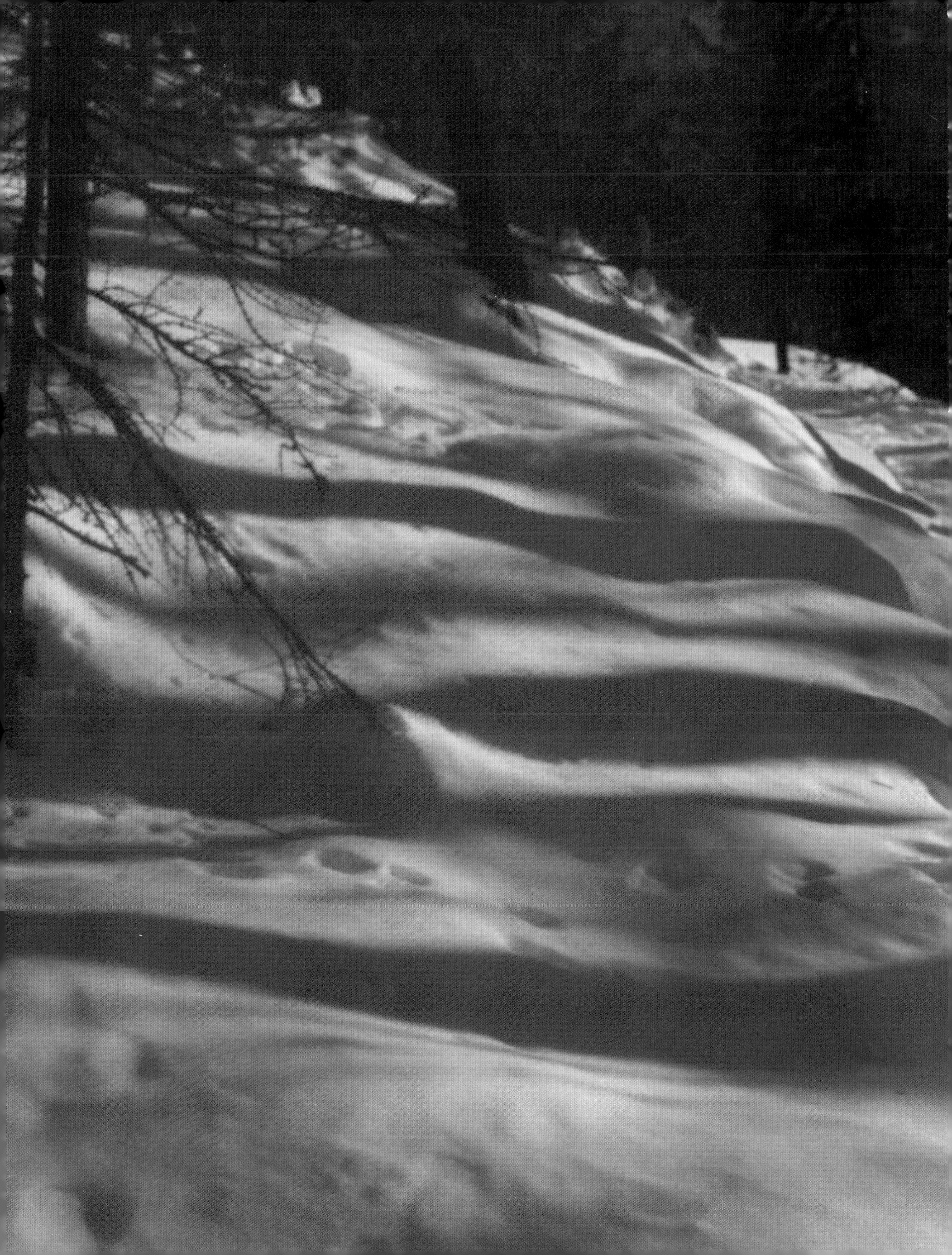

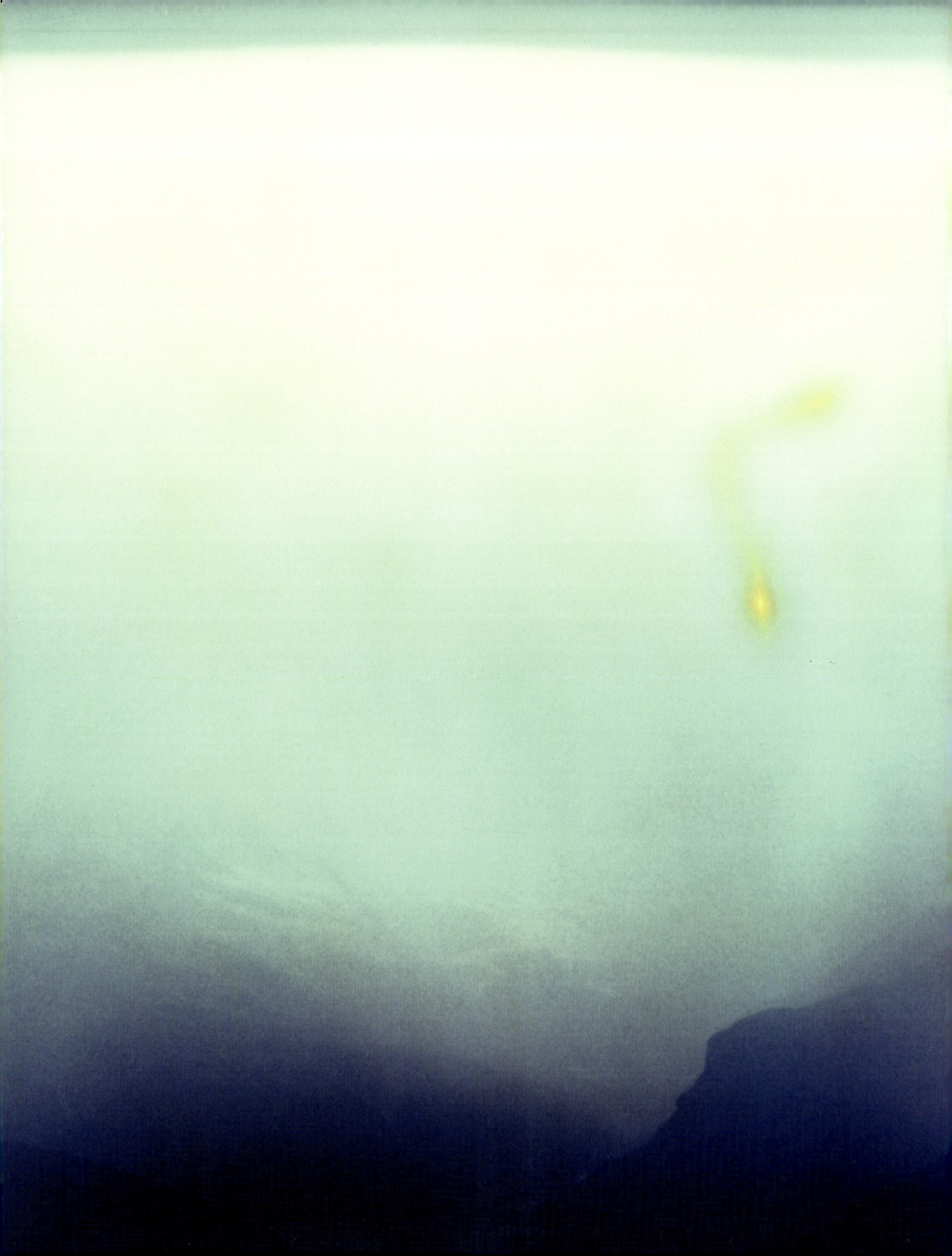

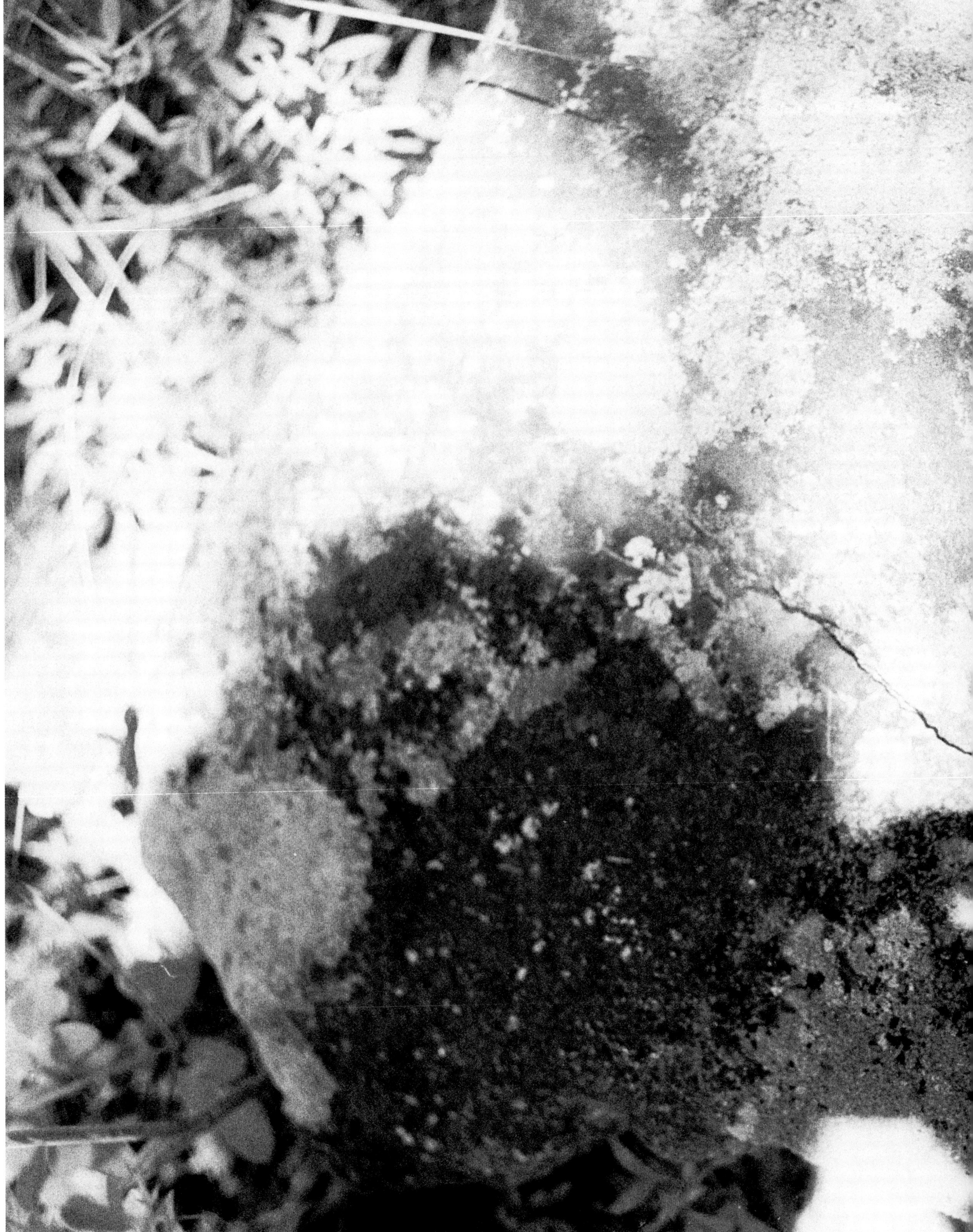

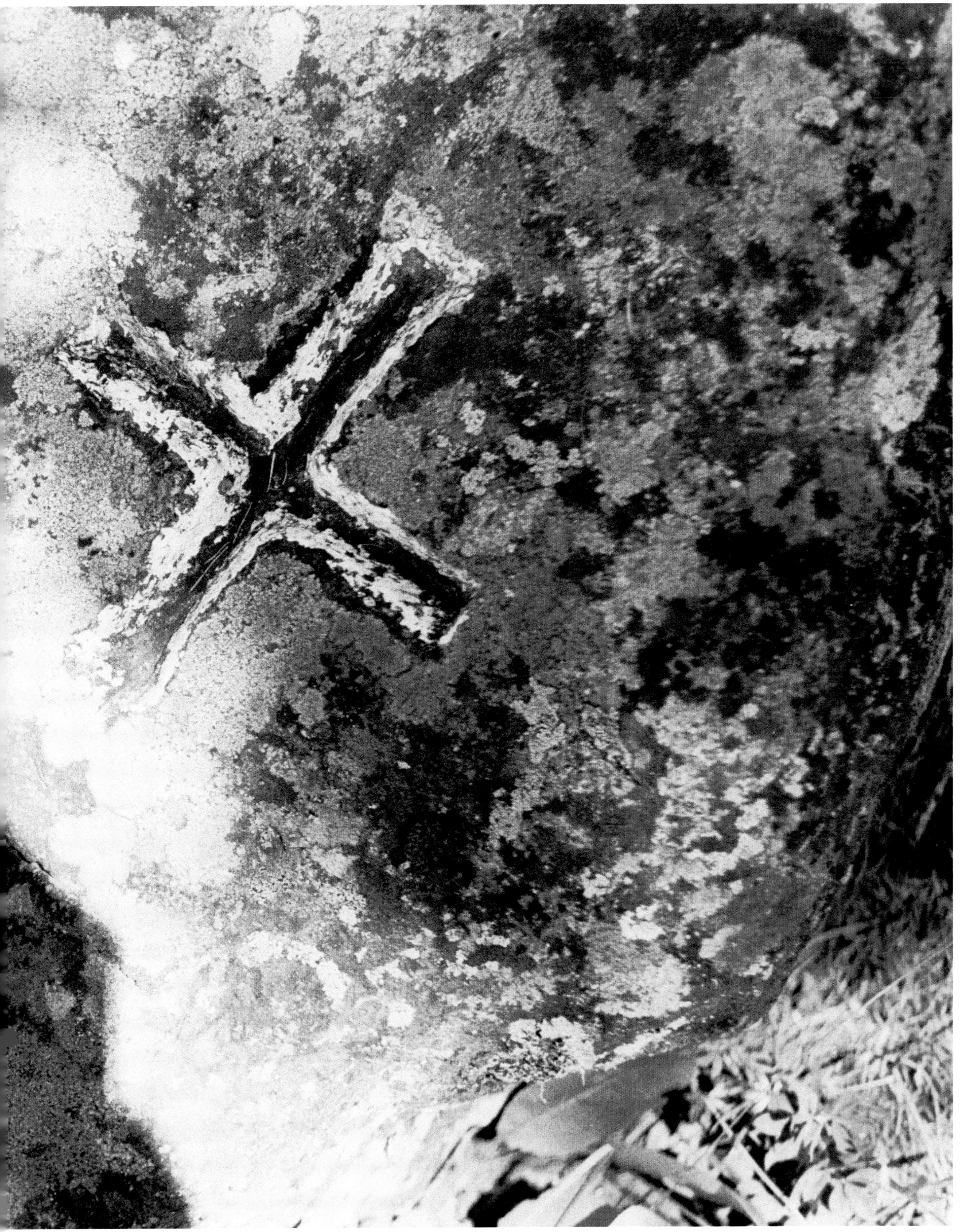

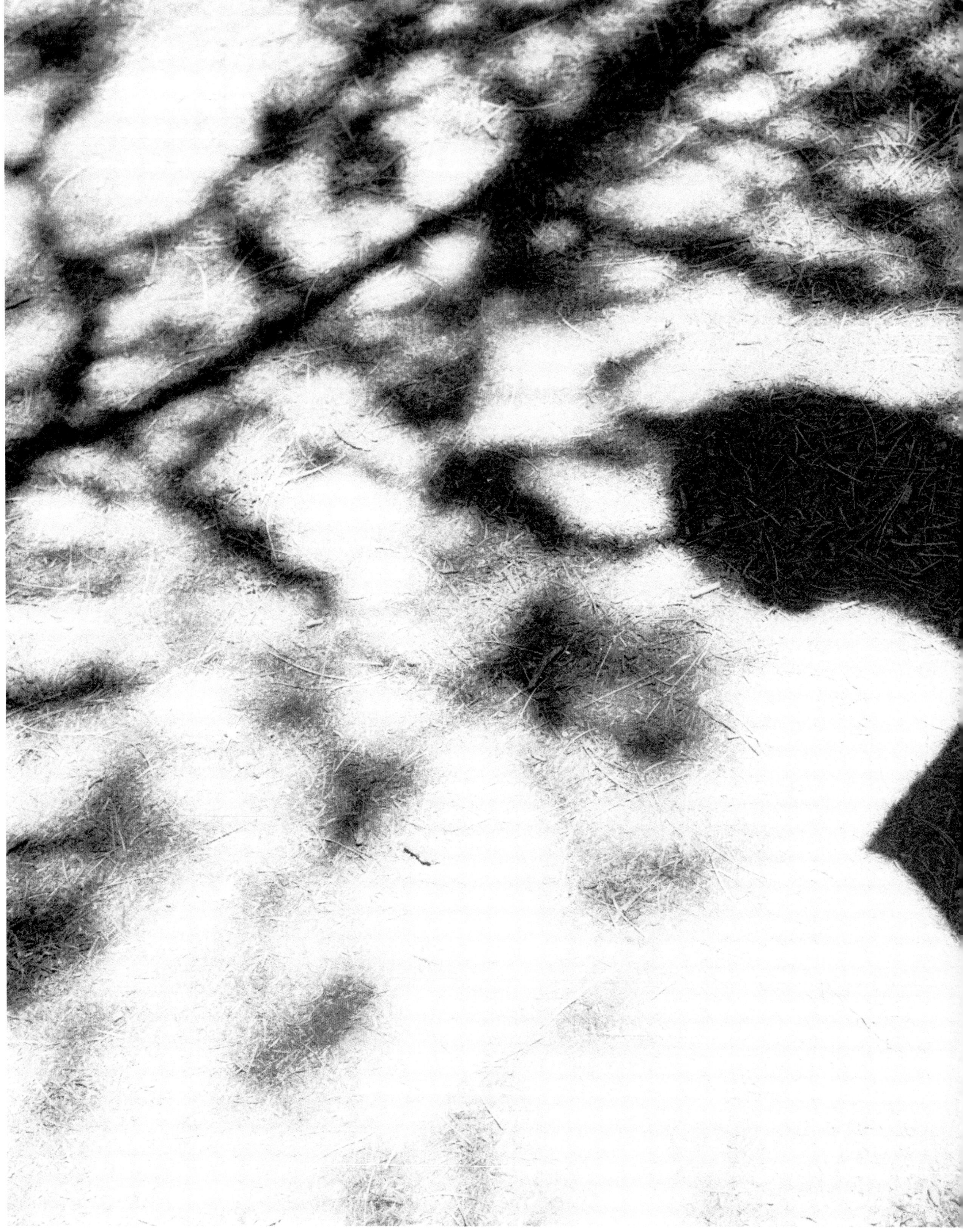

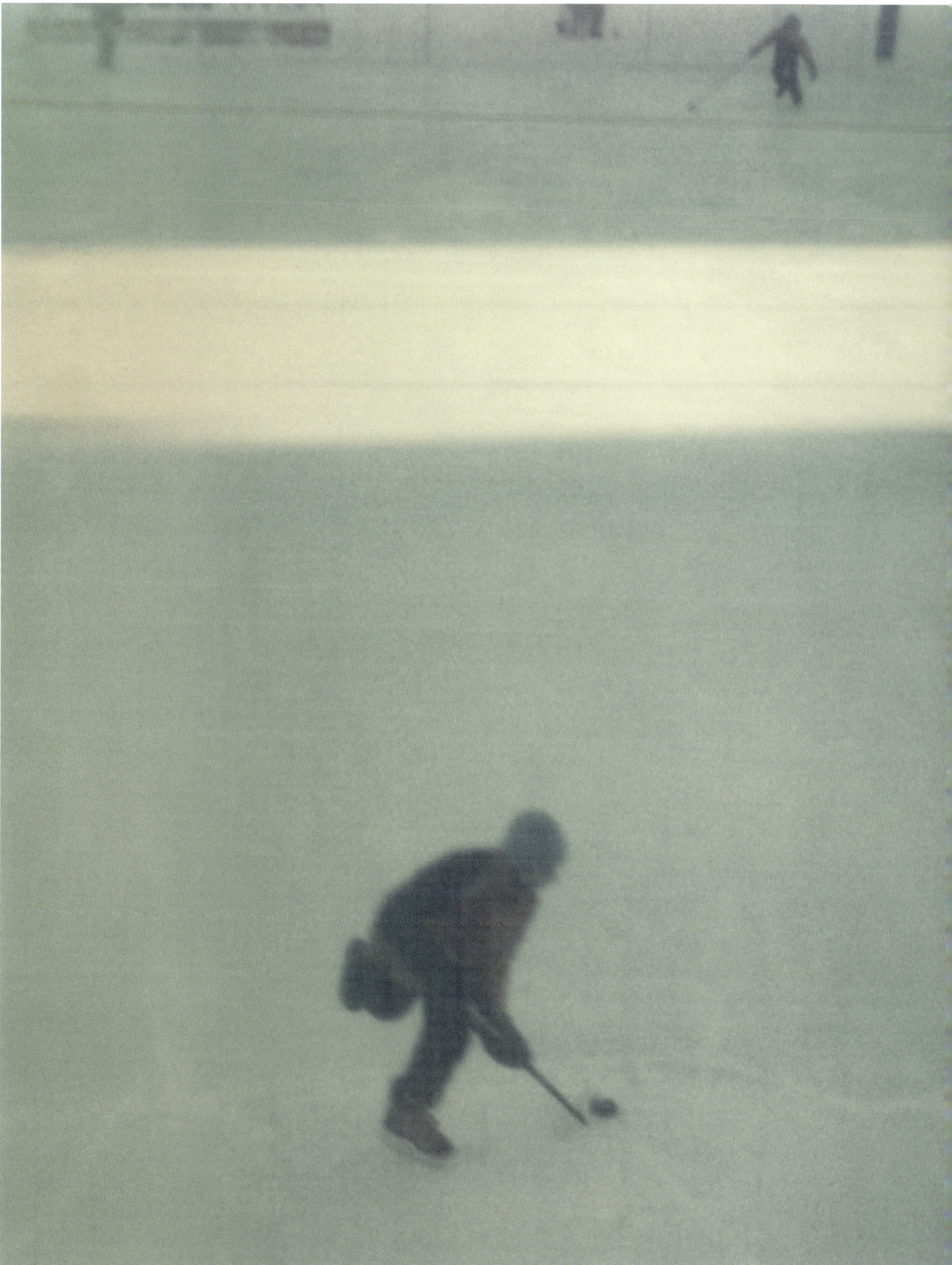

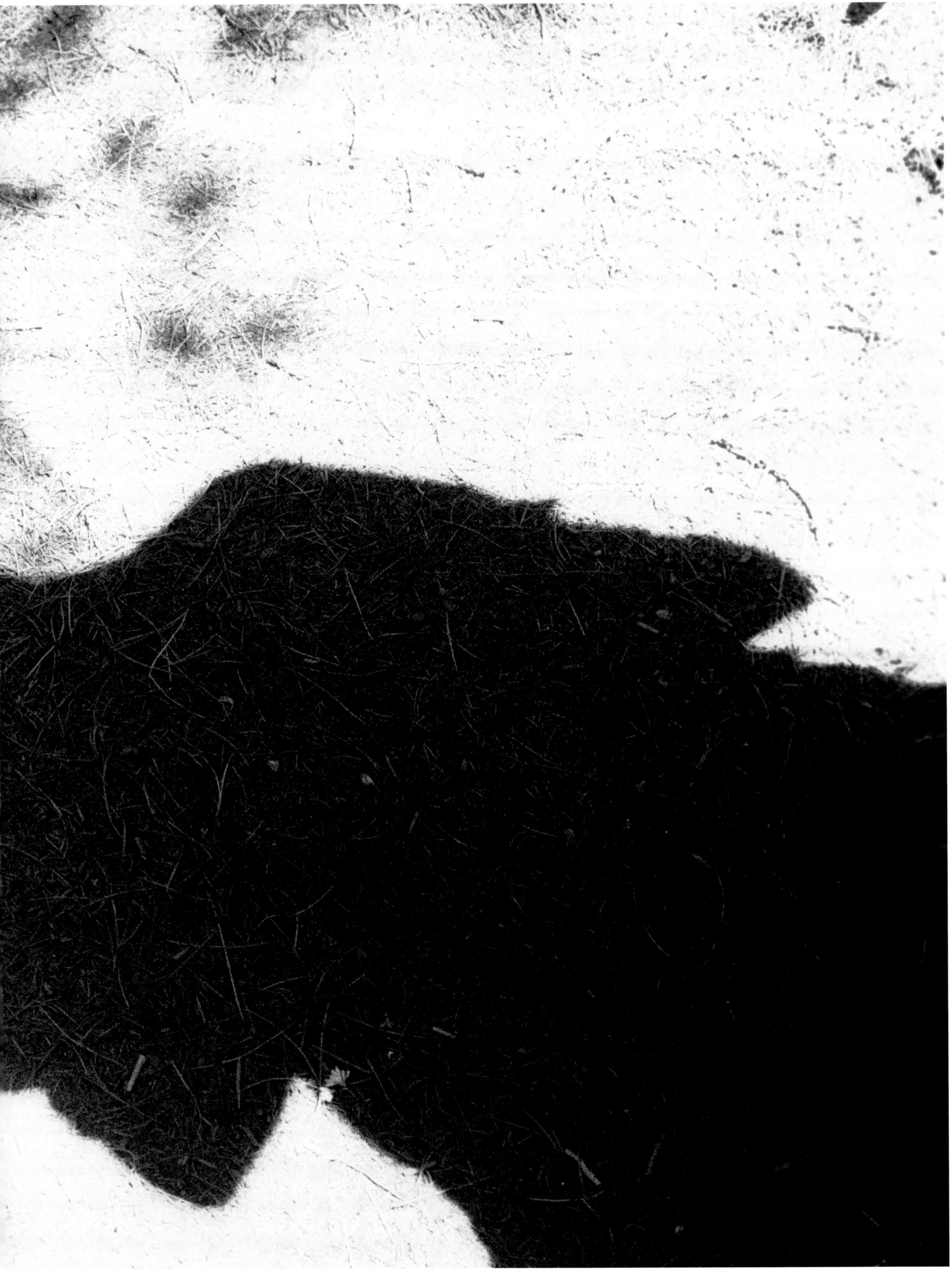

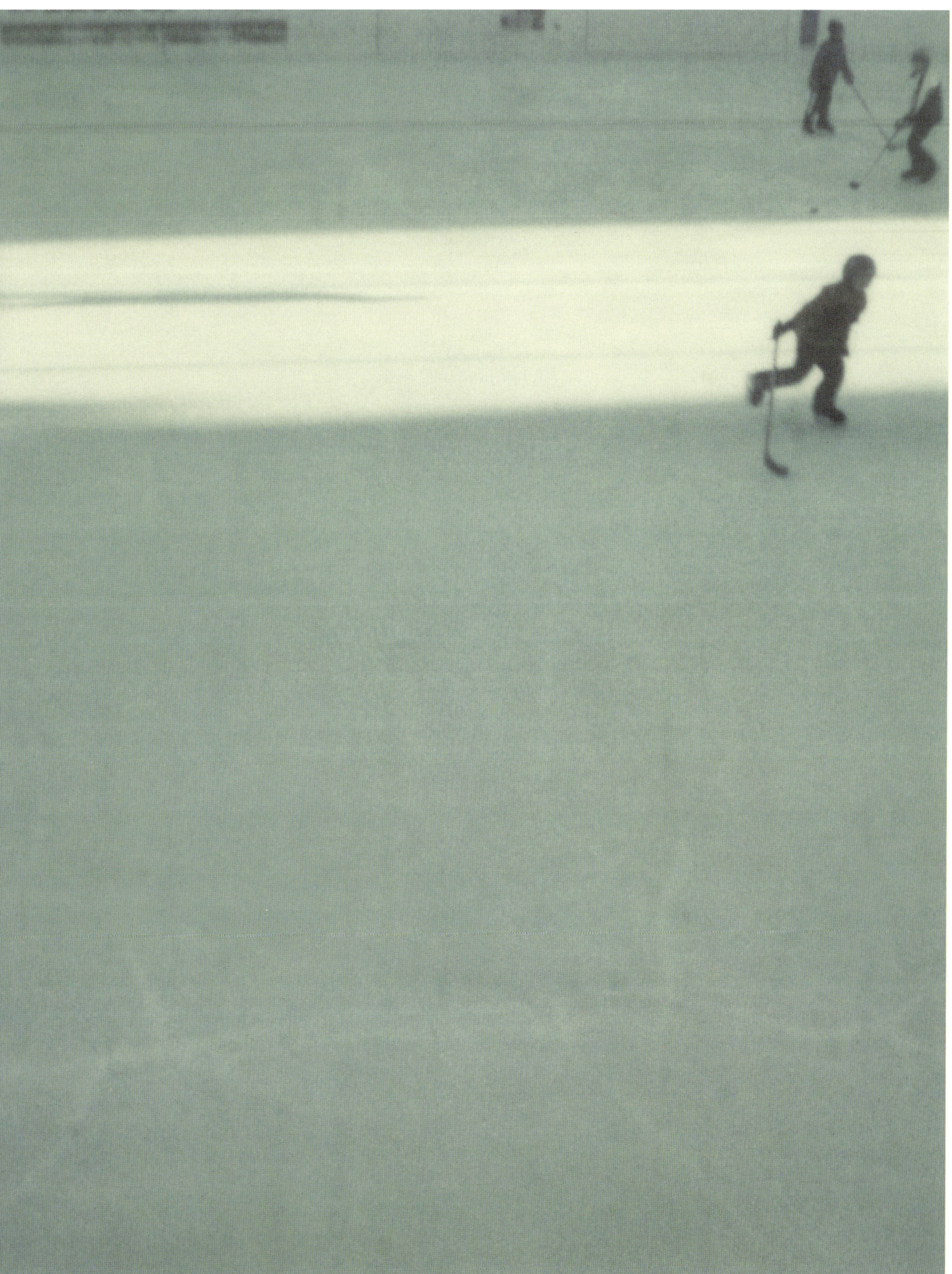

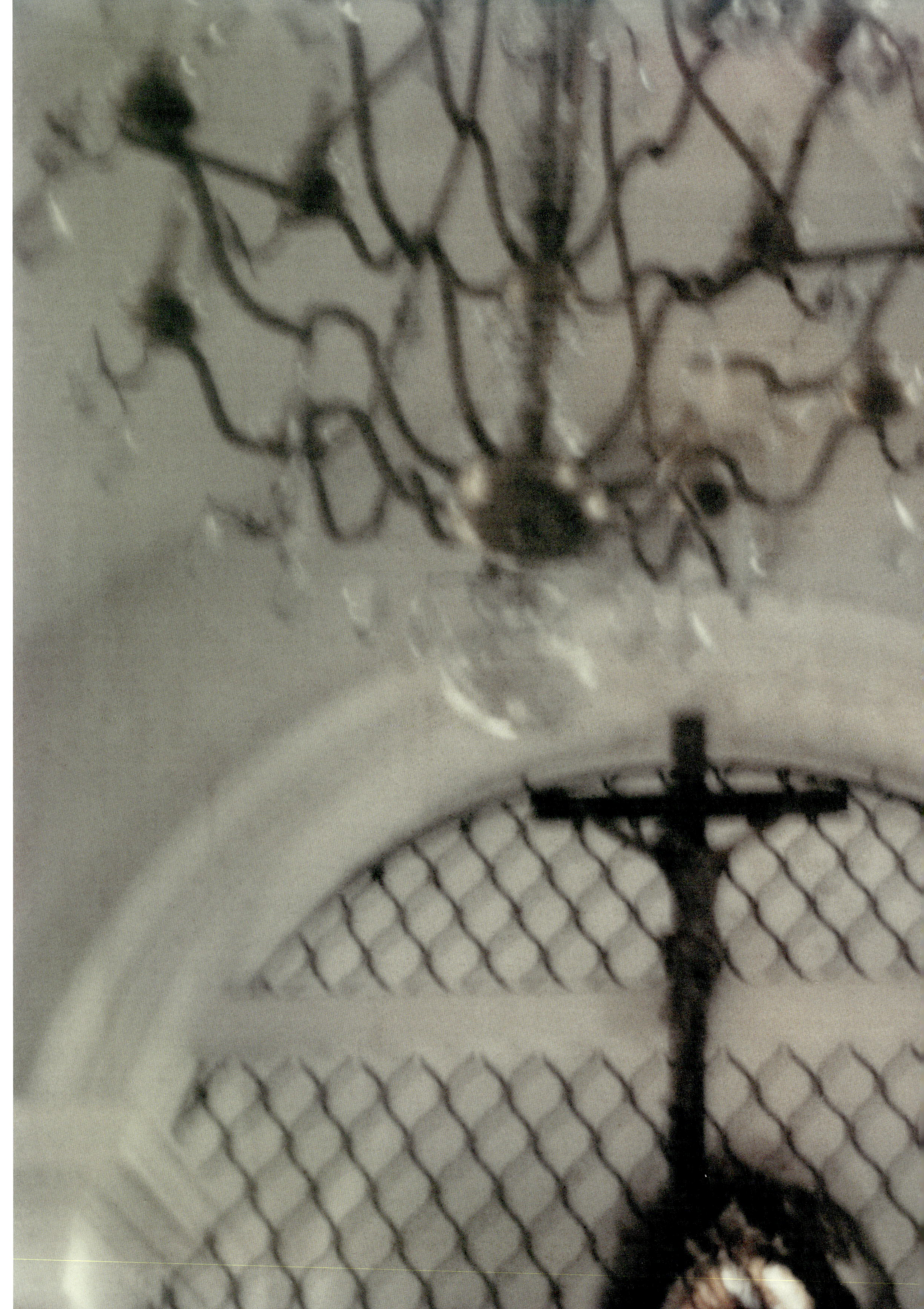

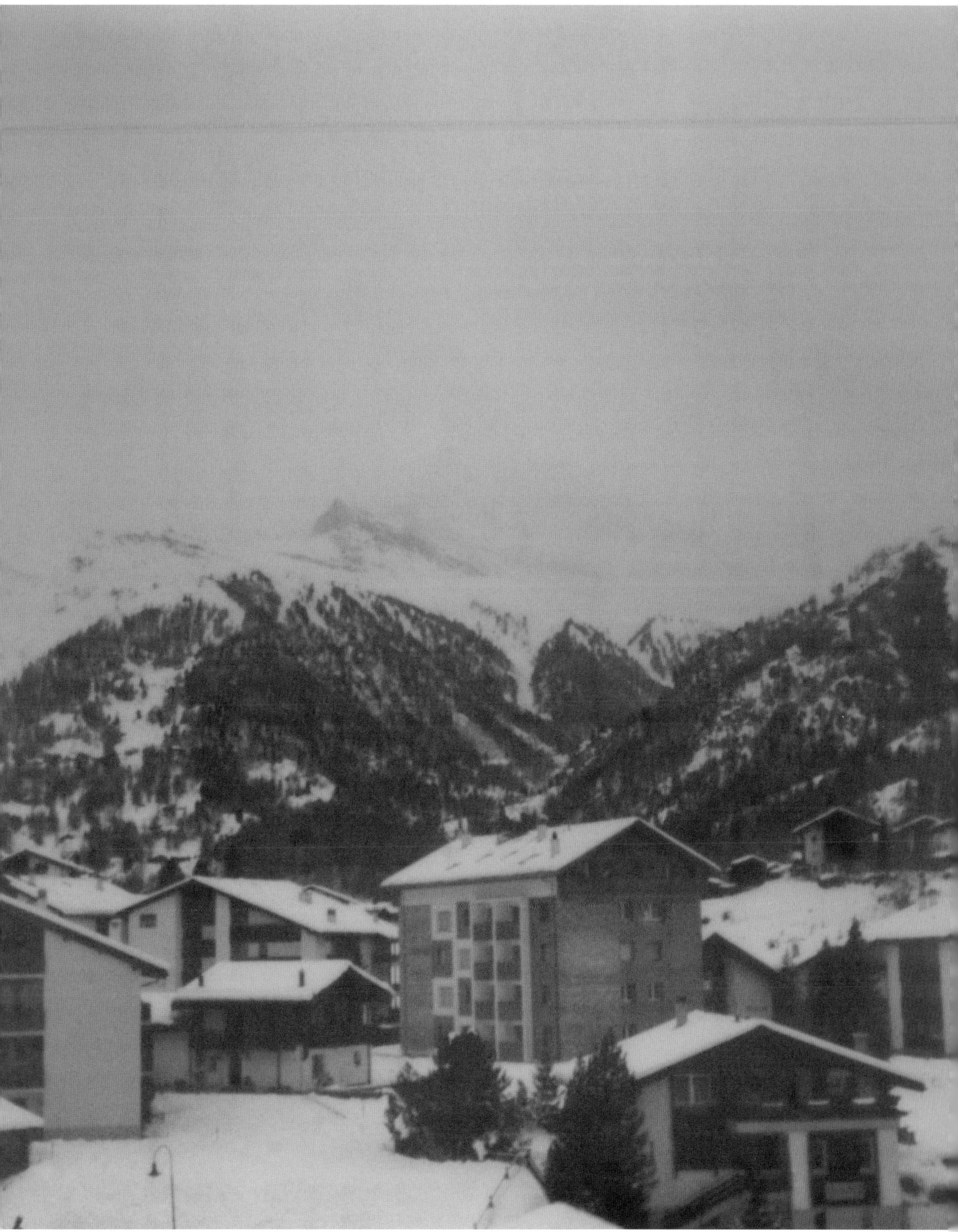

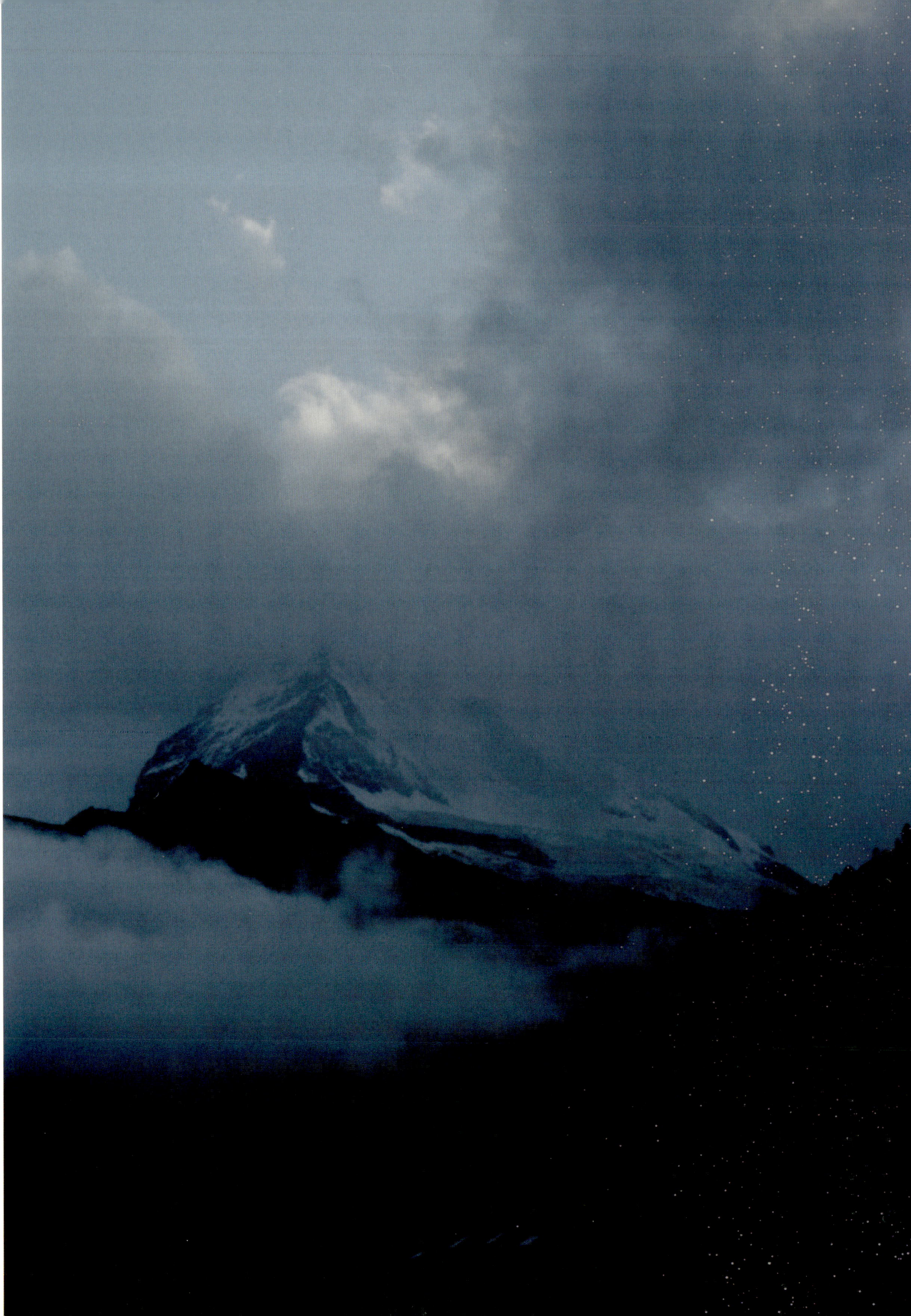

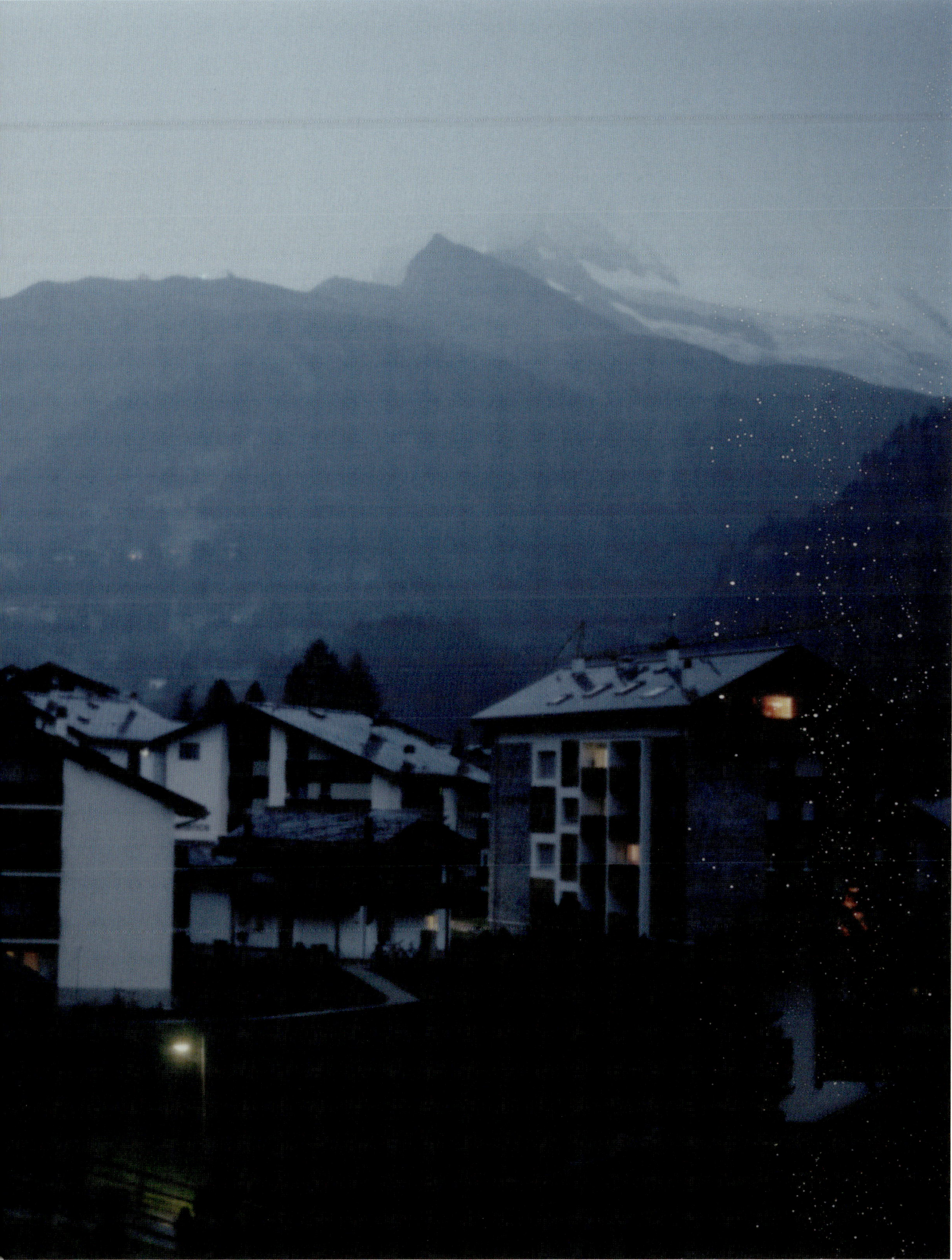

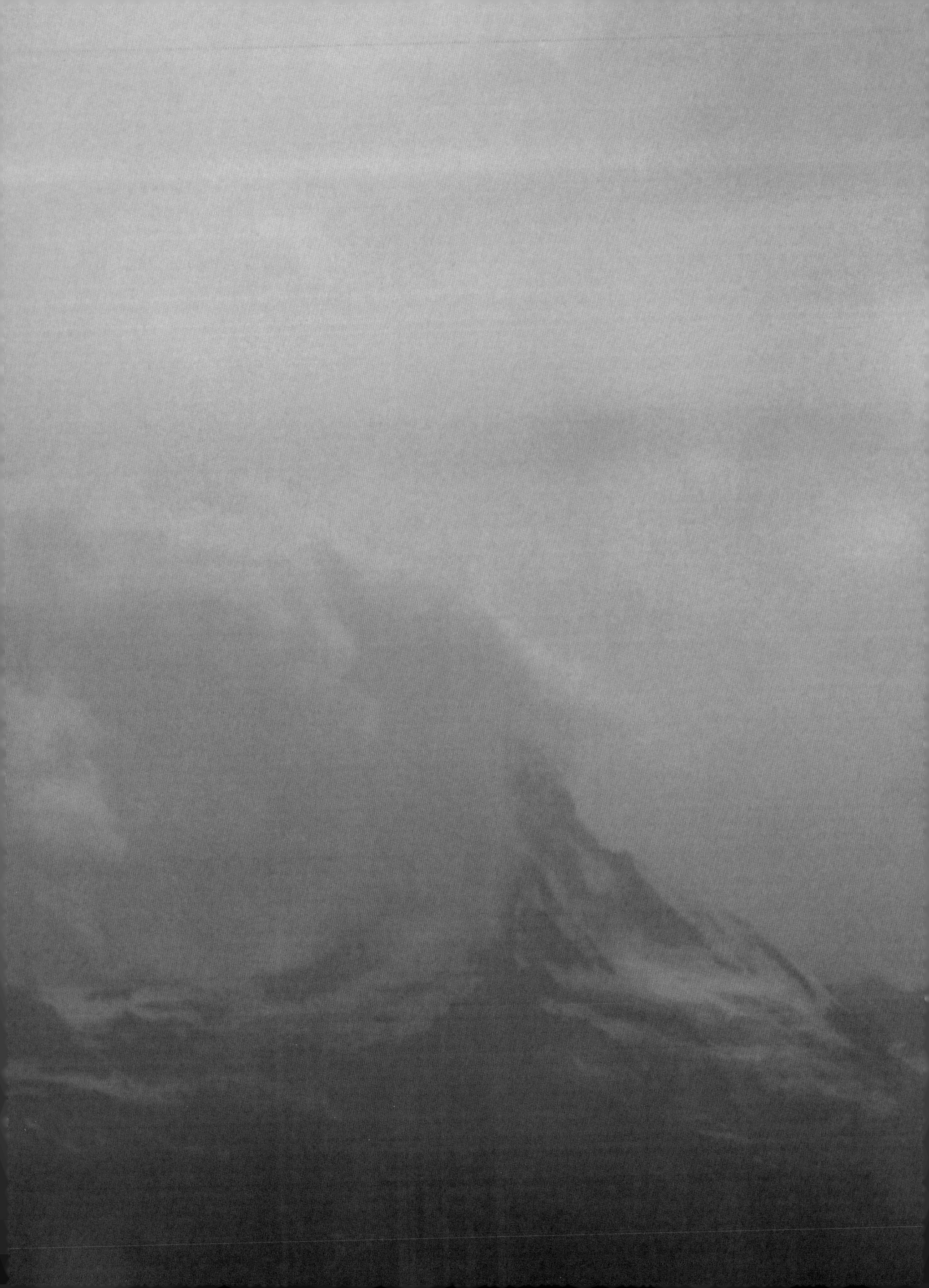

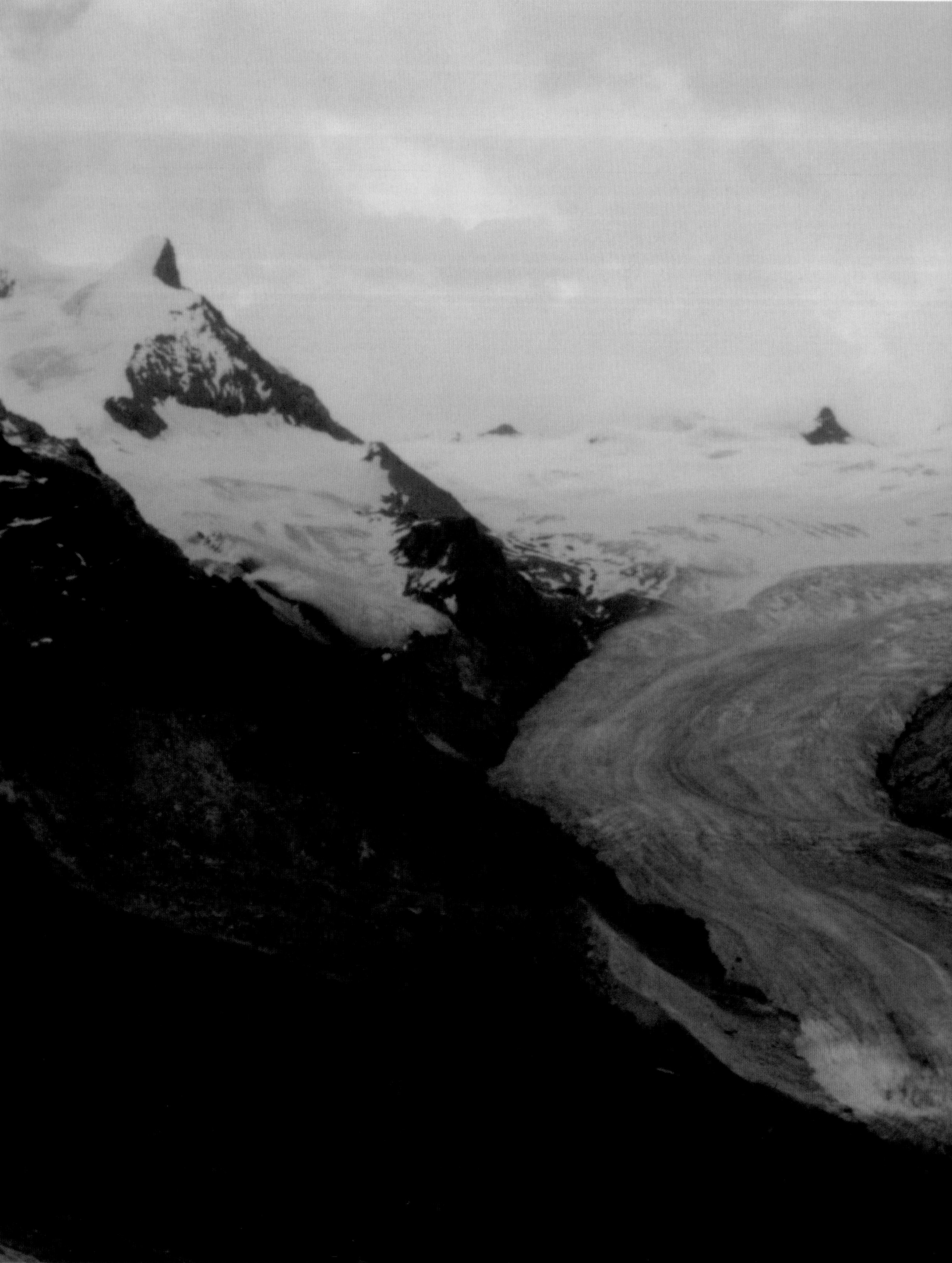

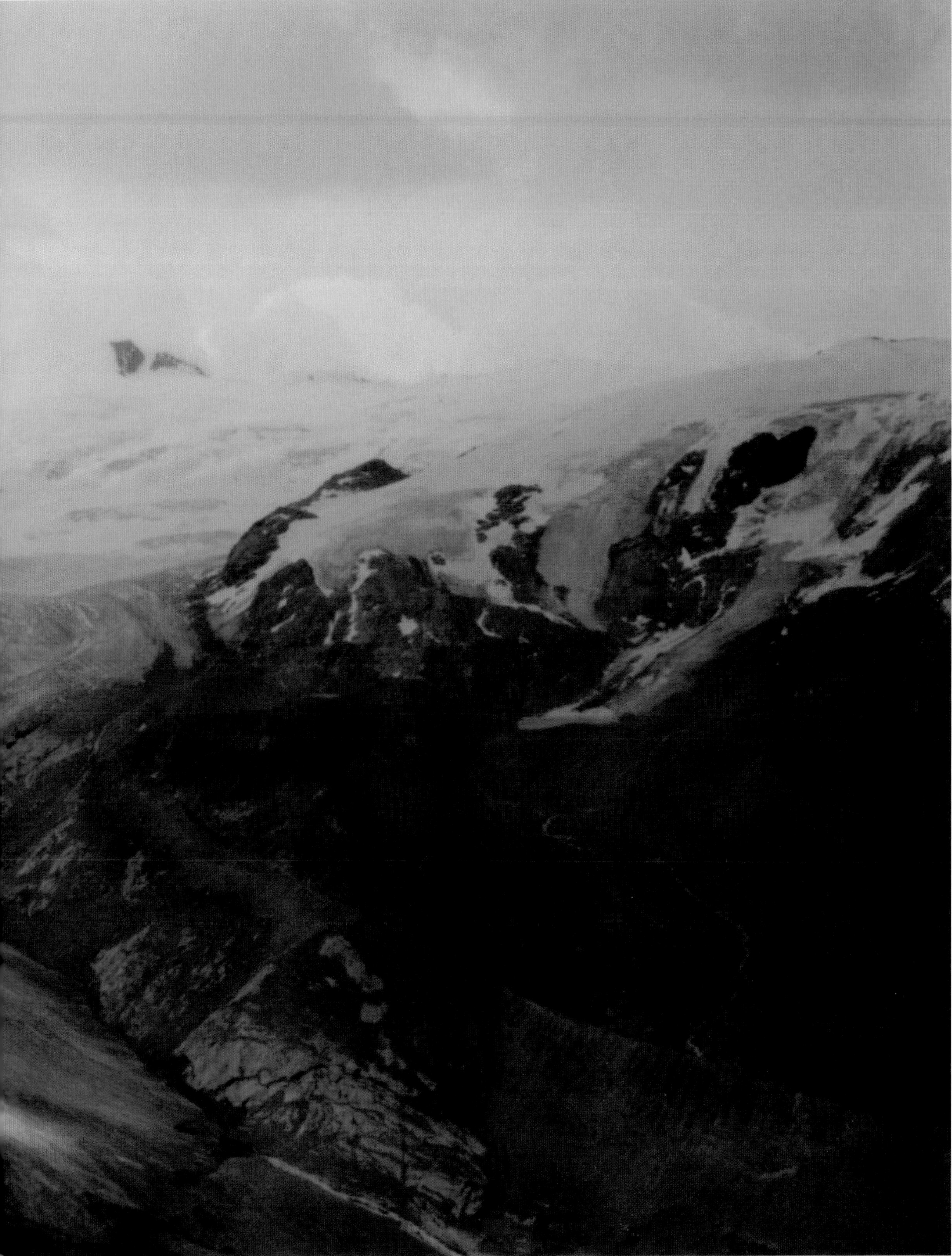

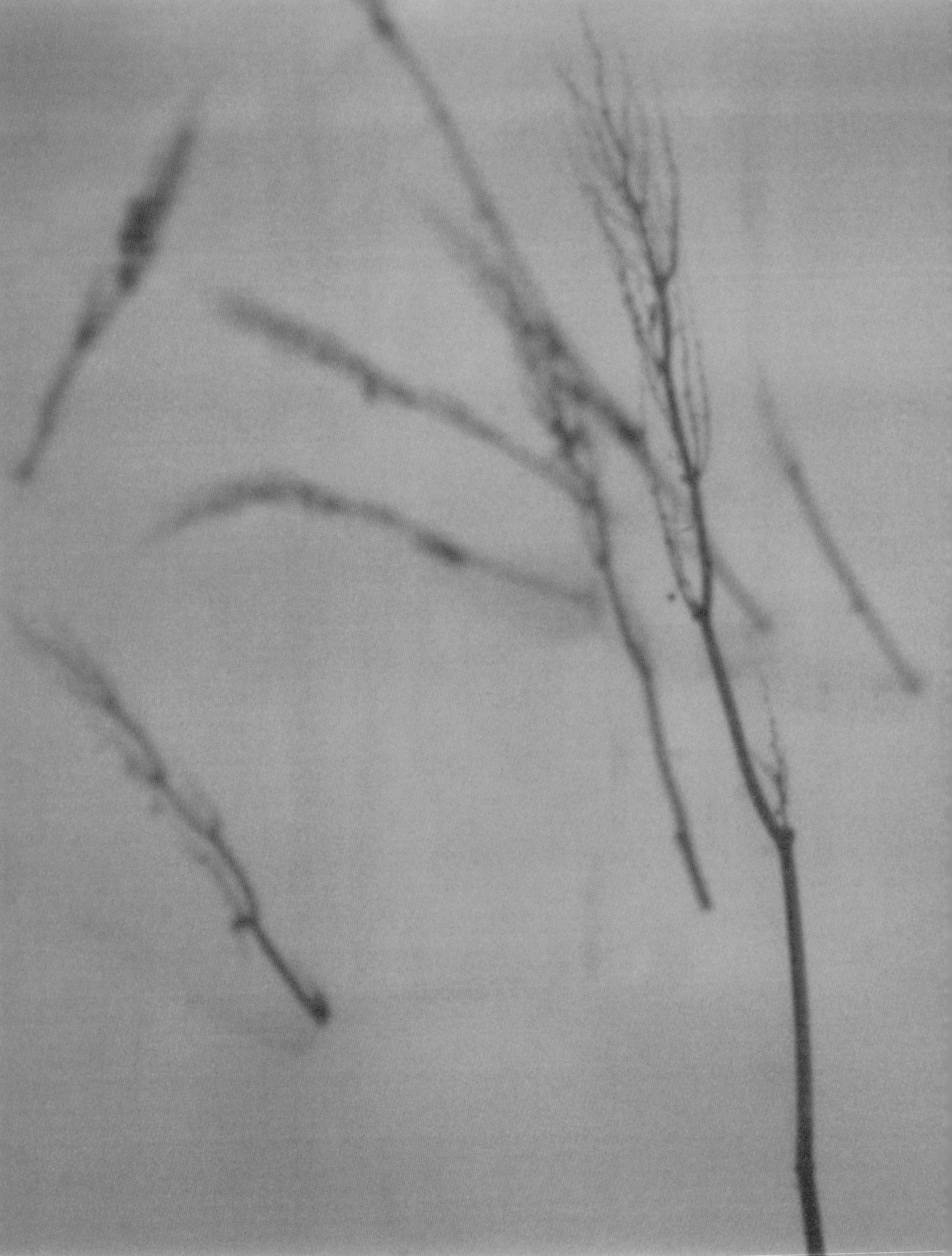

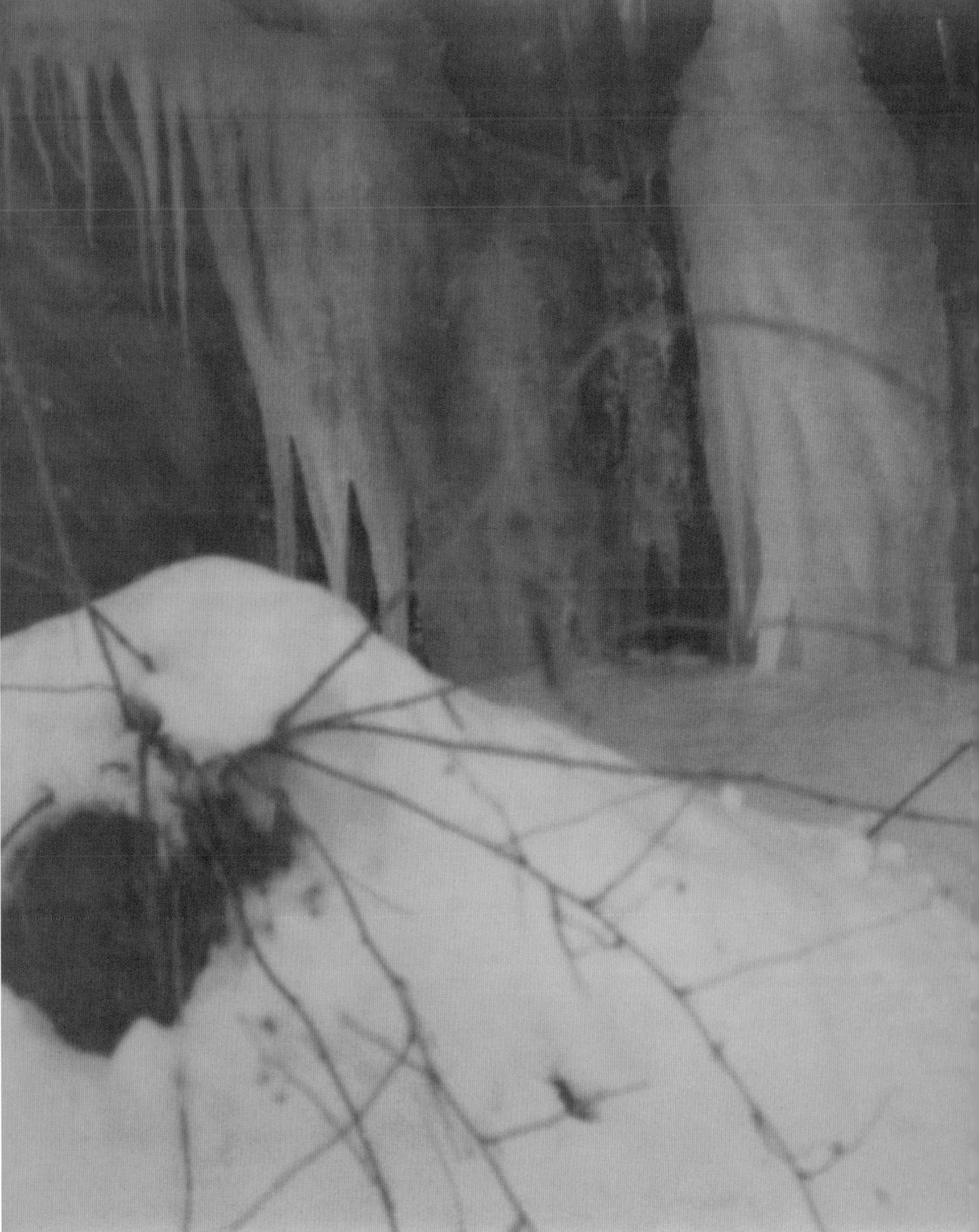

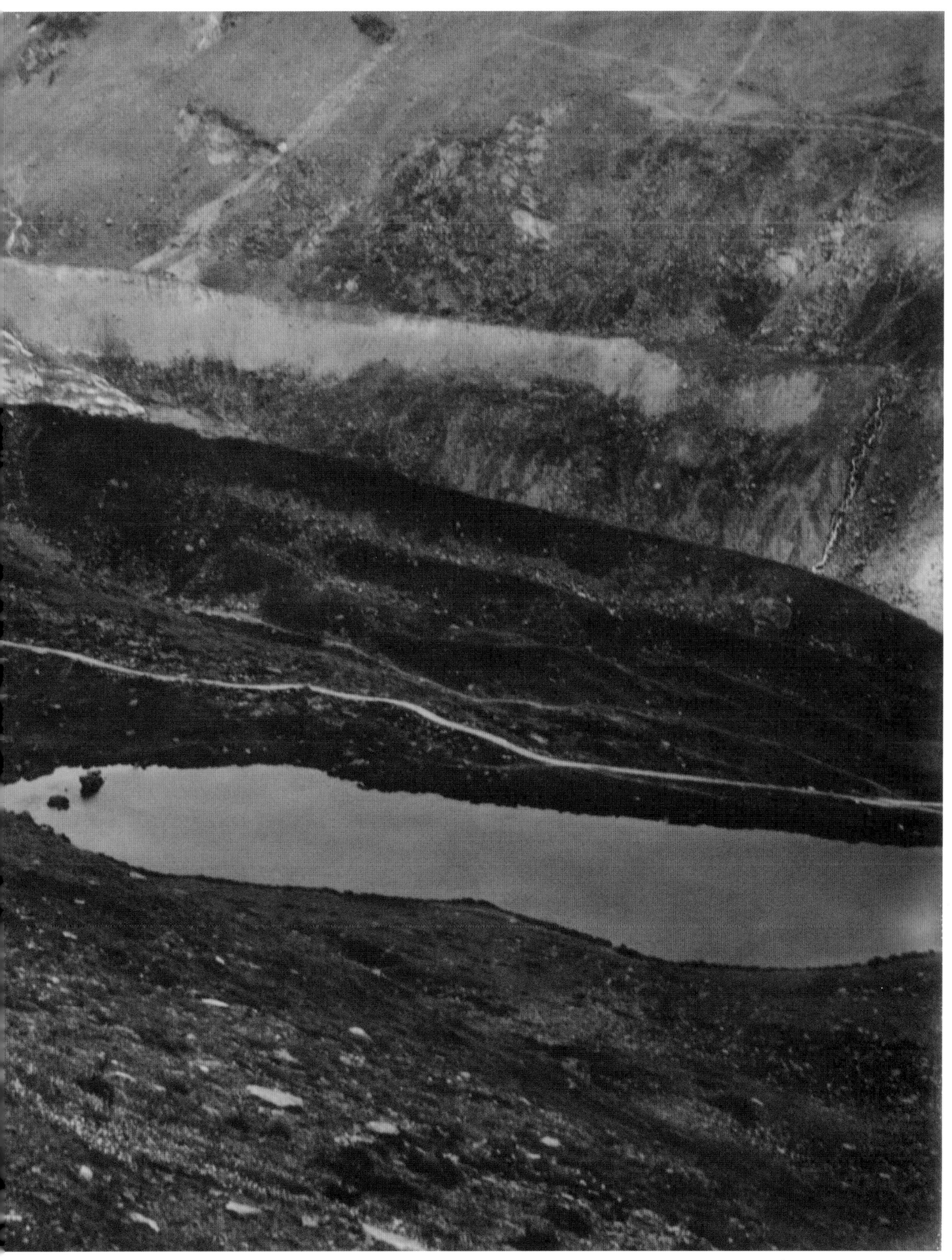

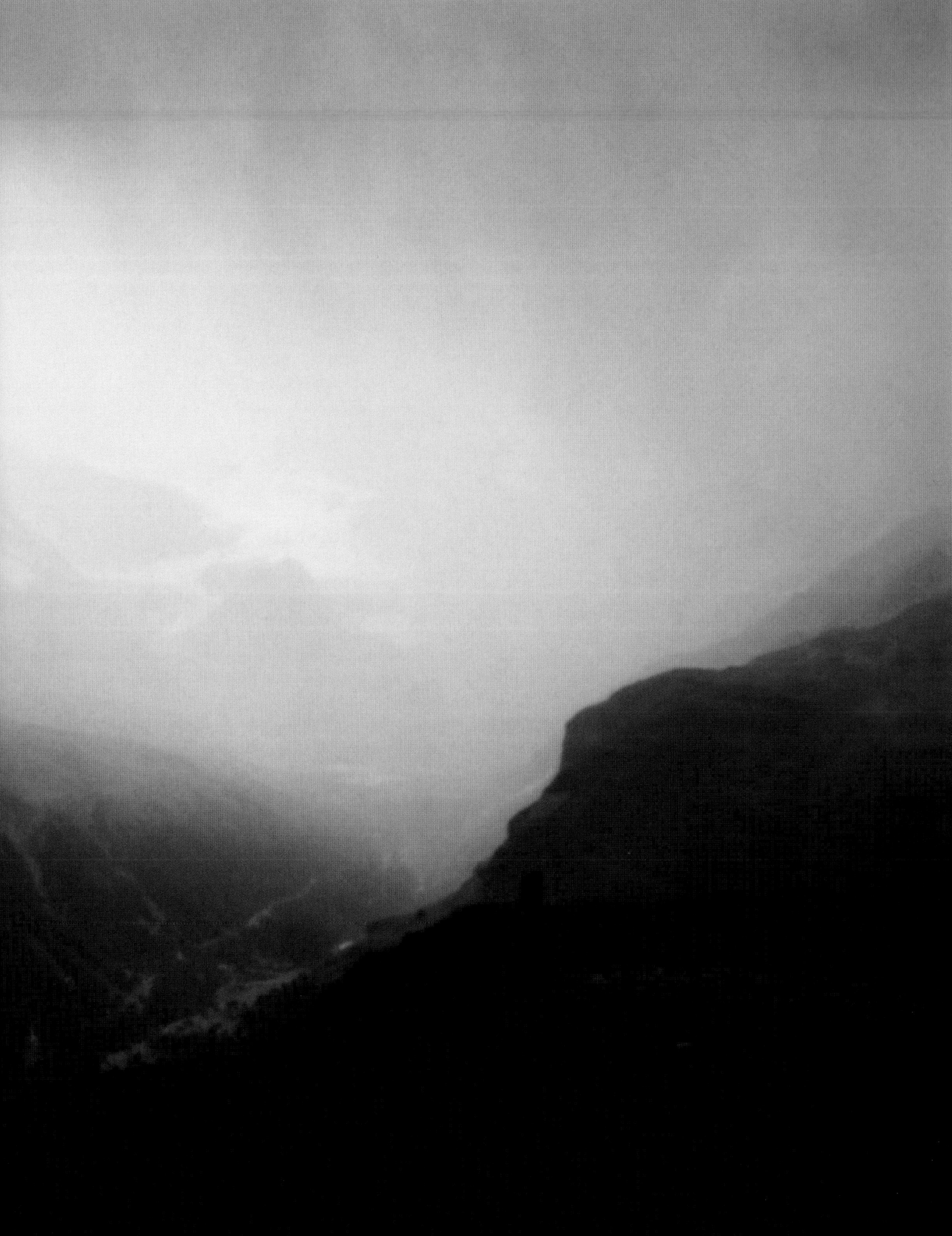

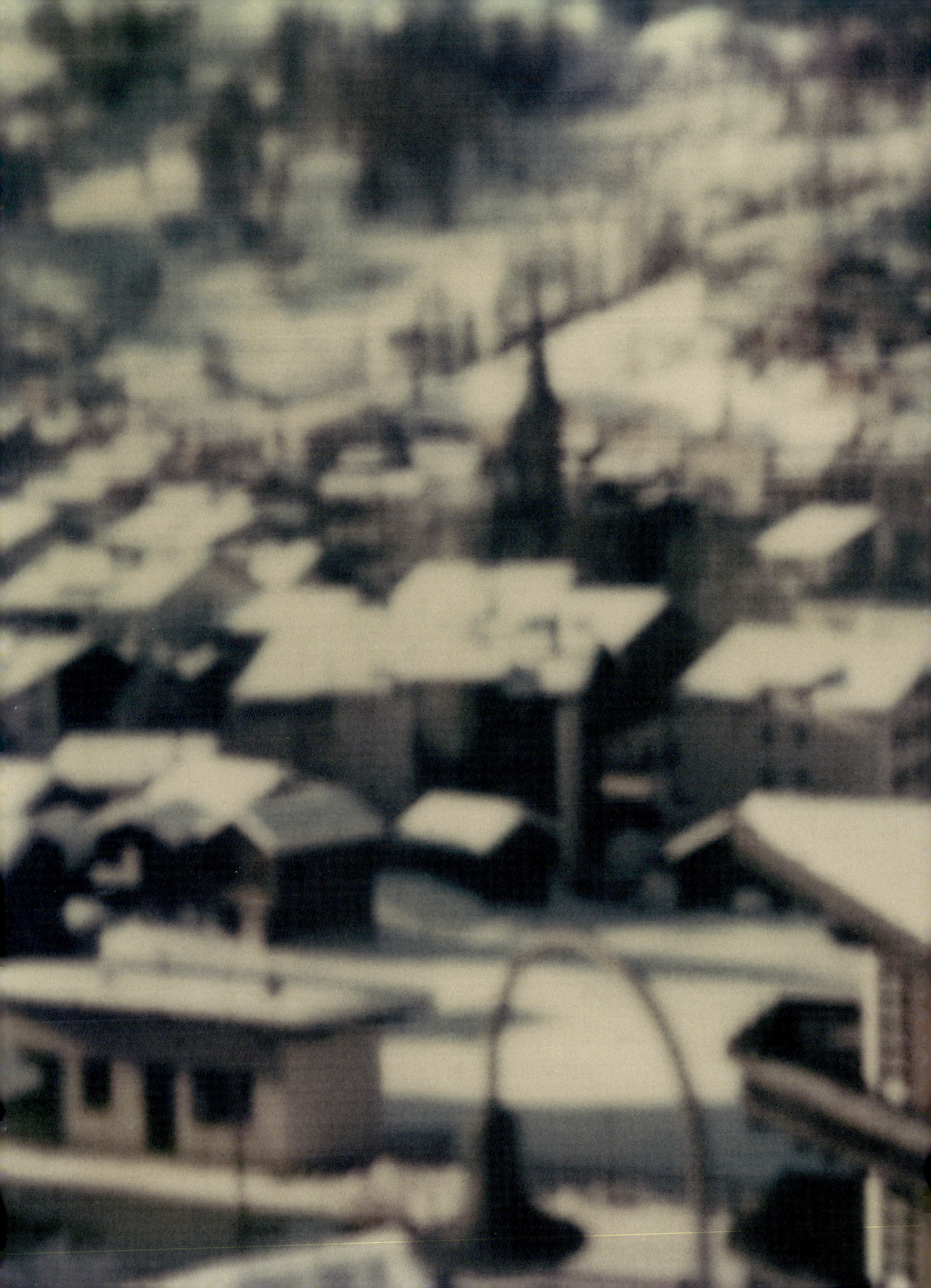

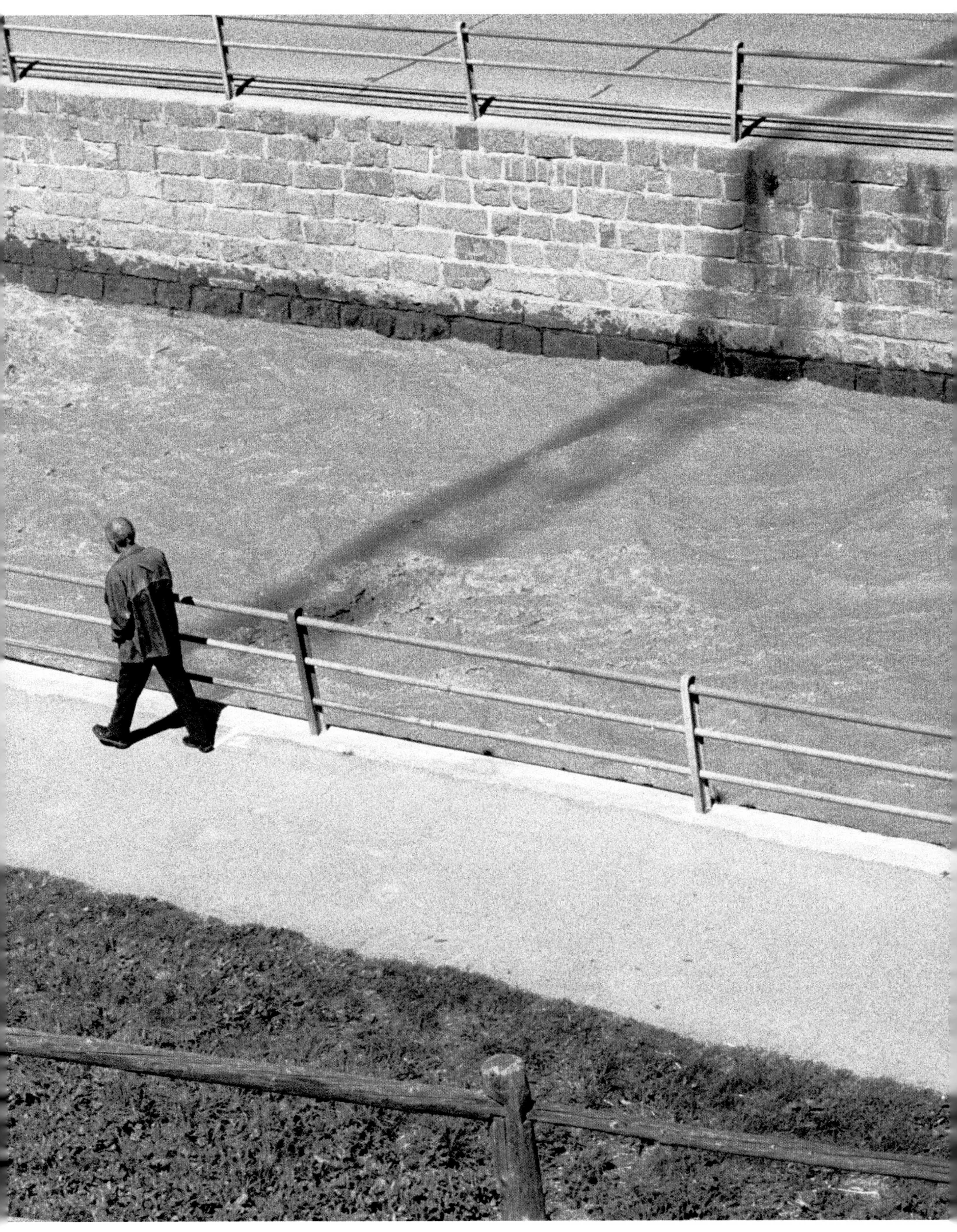

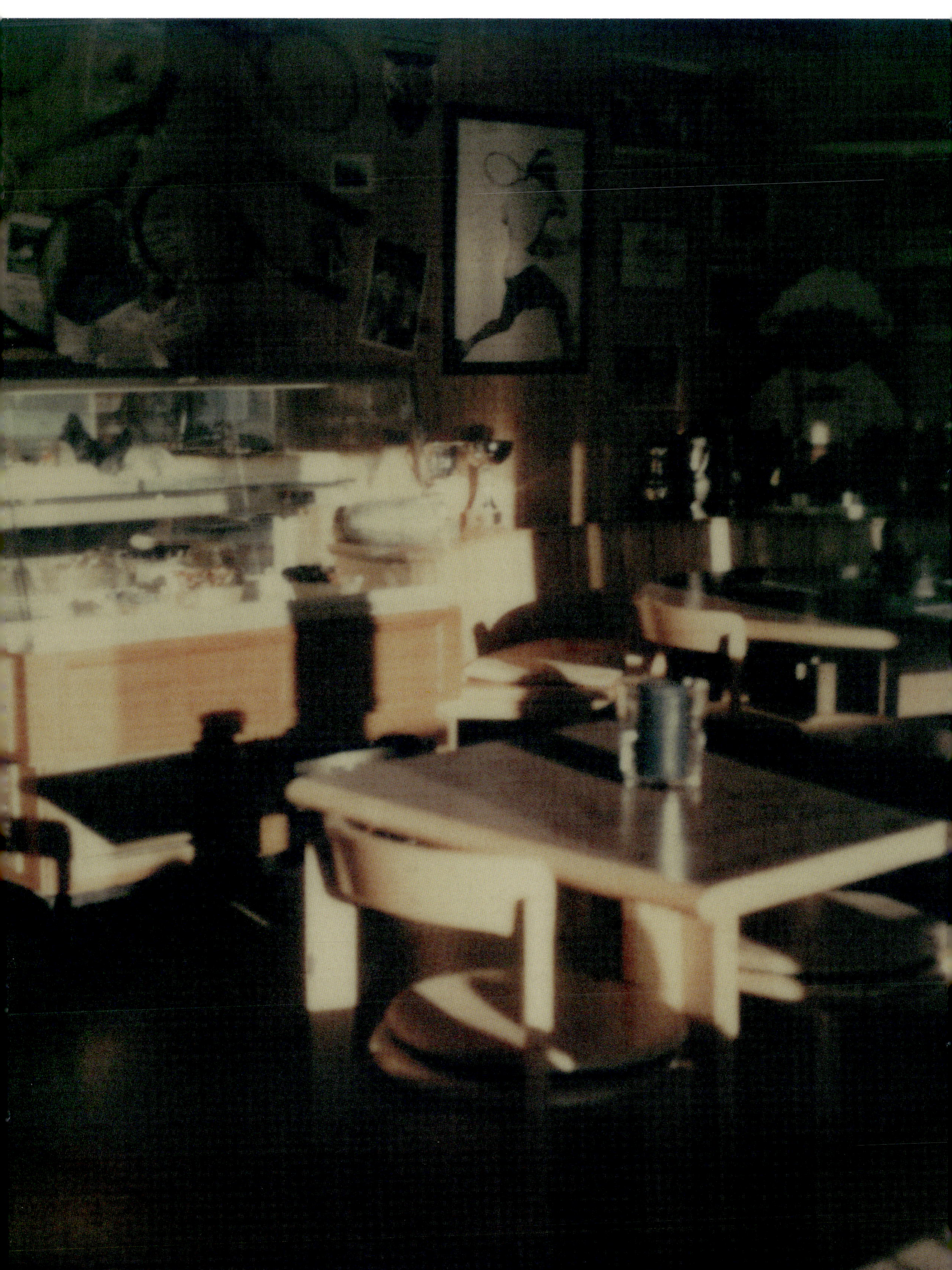

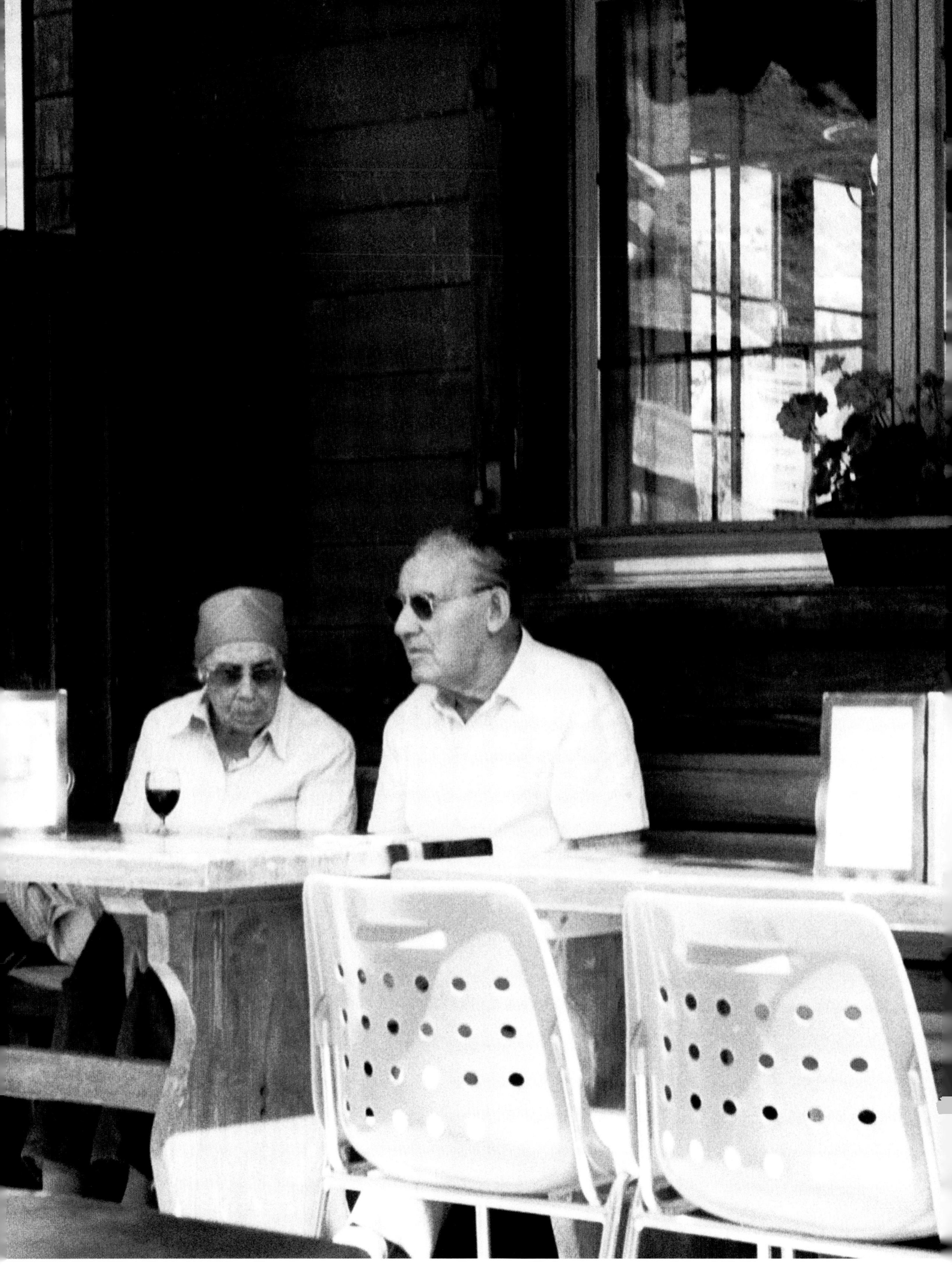

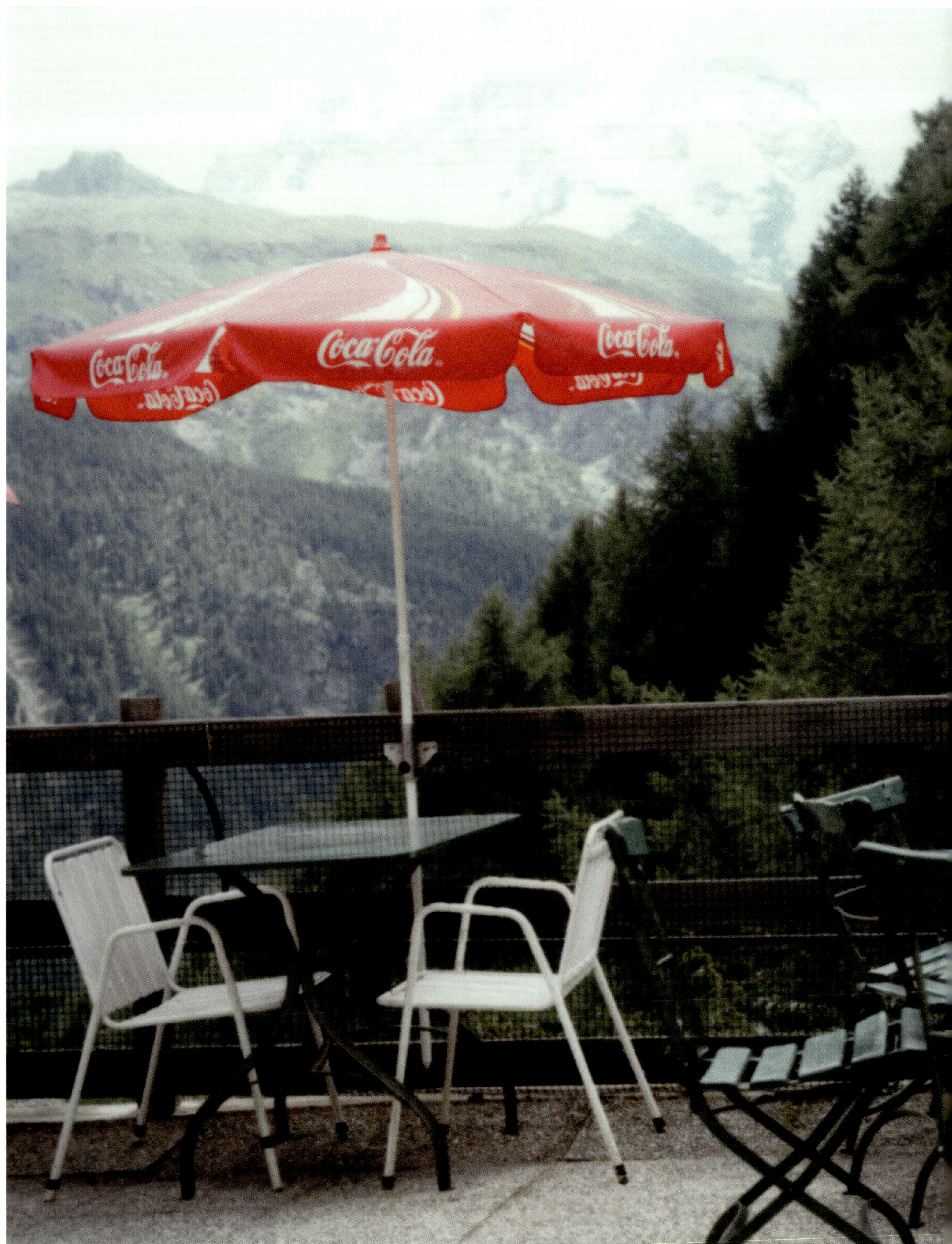

Coca-Cola.
Coca-Cola.
Coca-Cola.

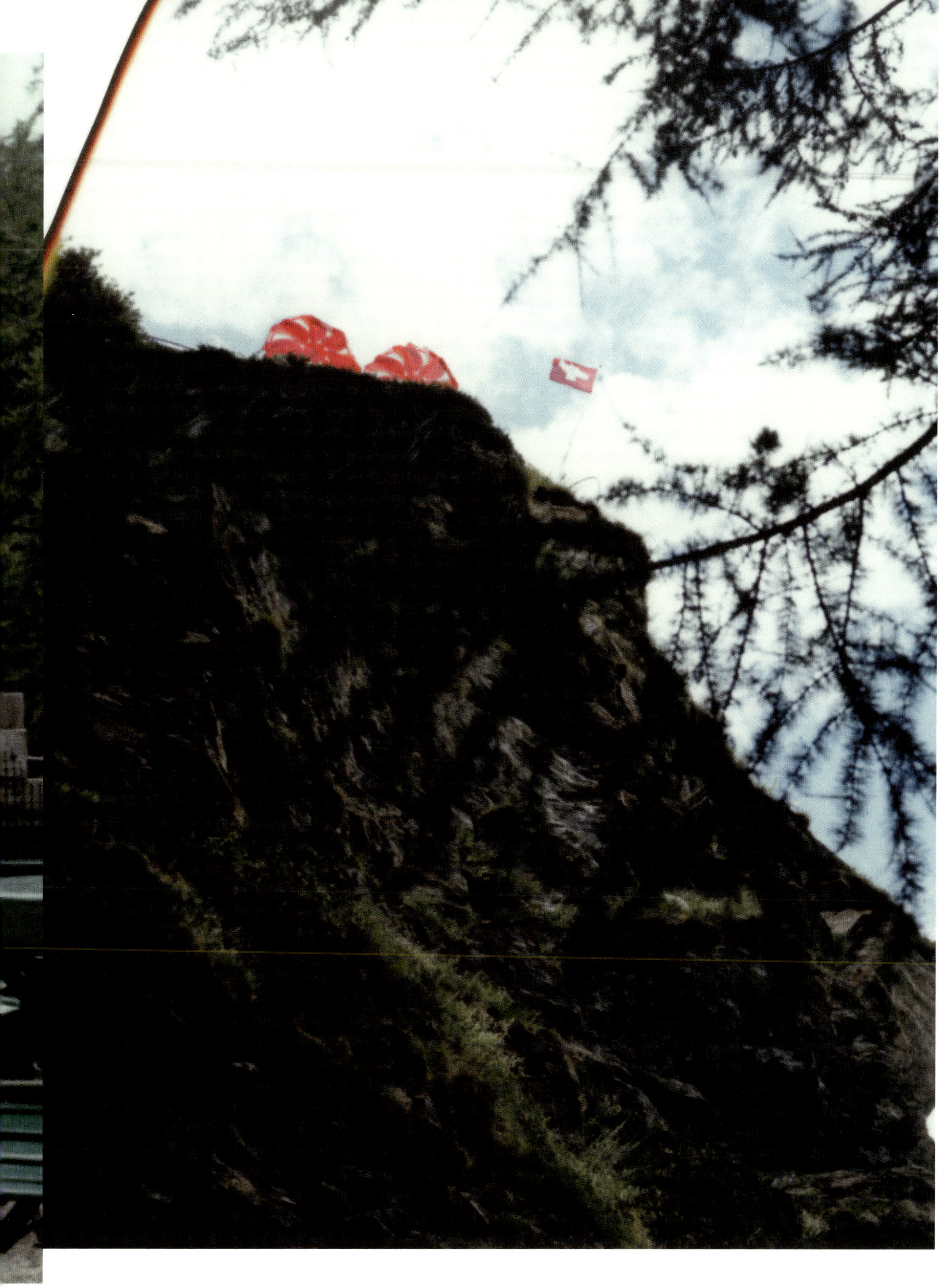

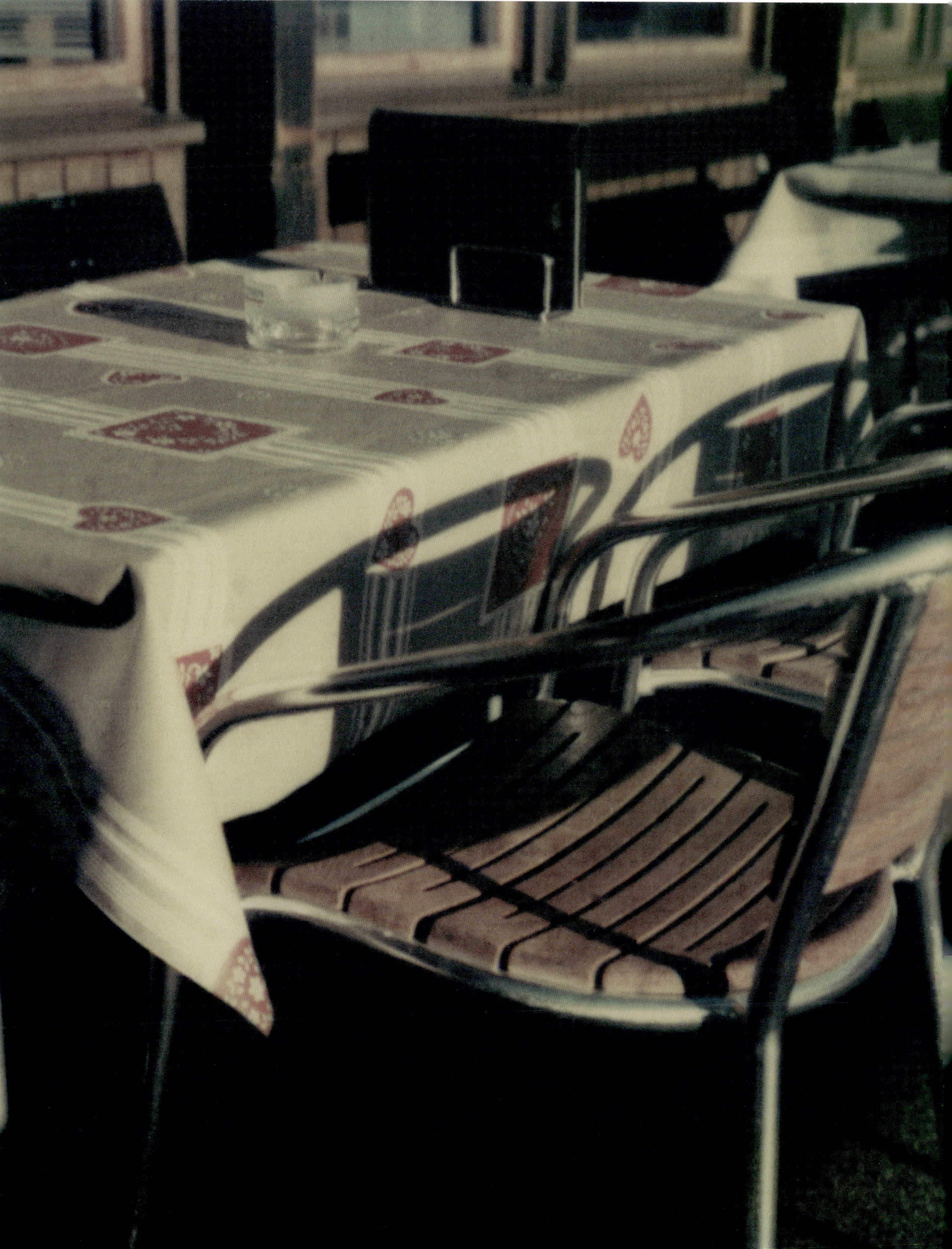

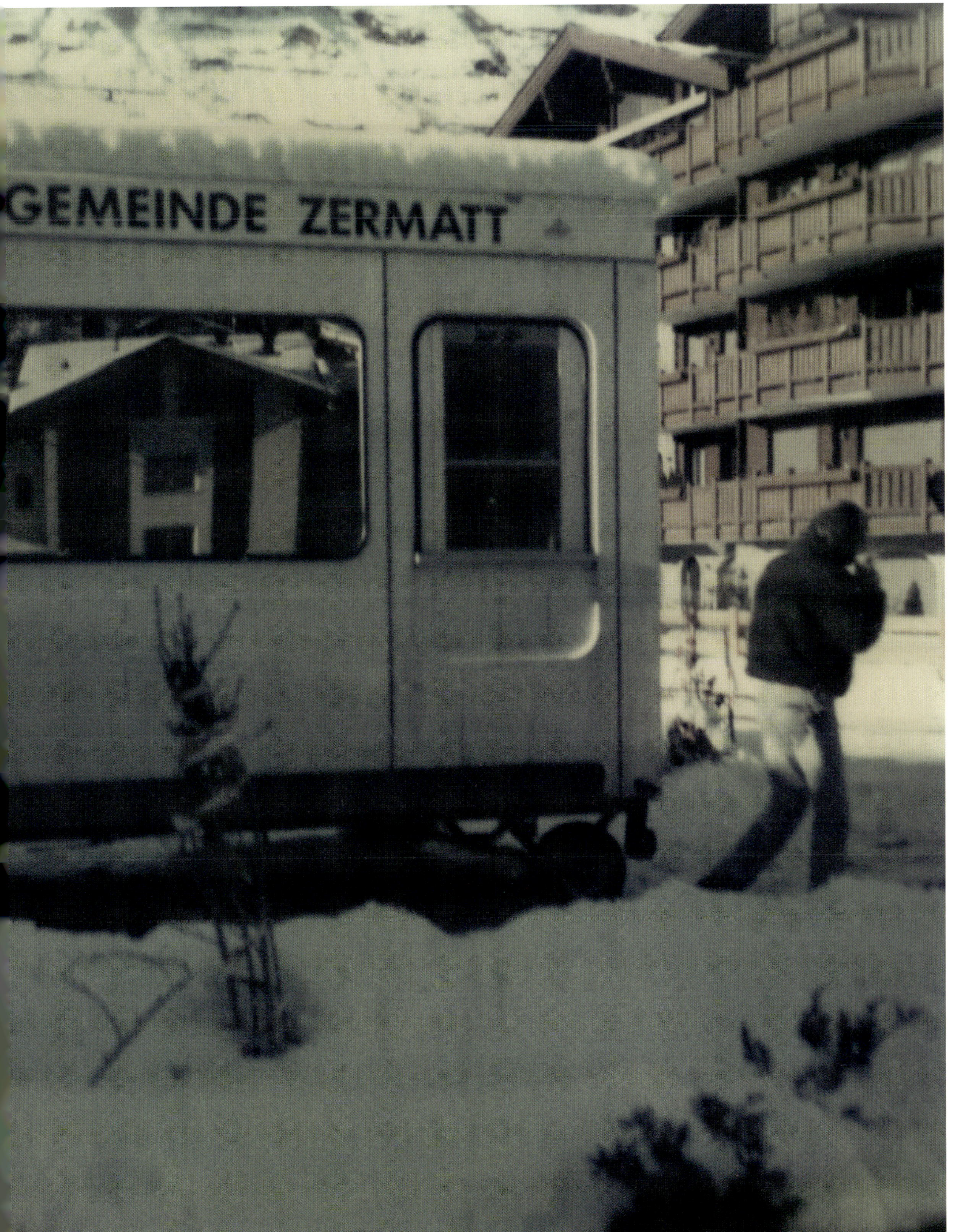
GEMEINDE ZERMATT

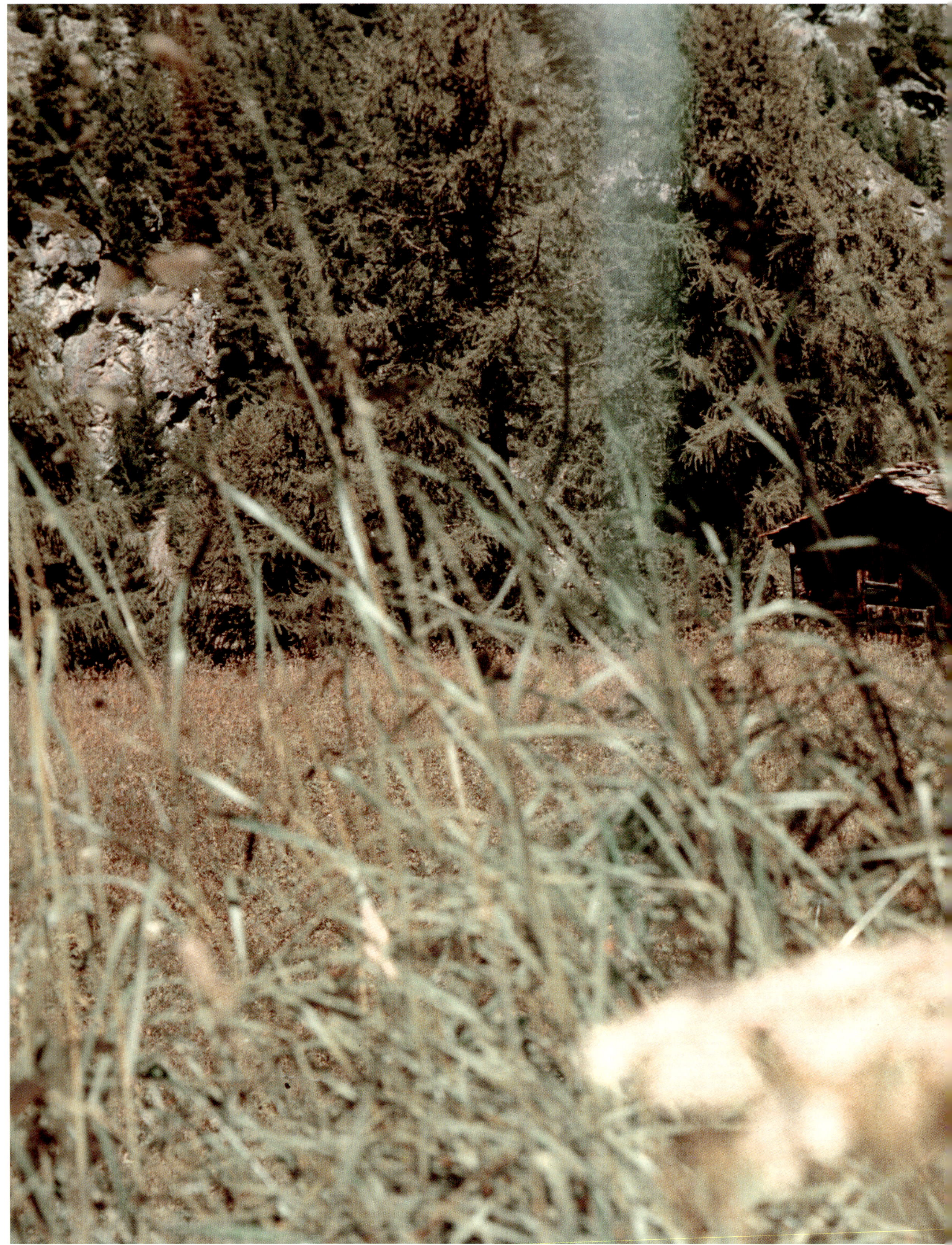

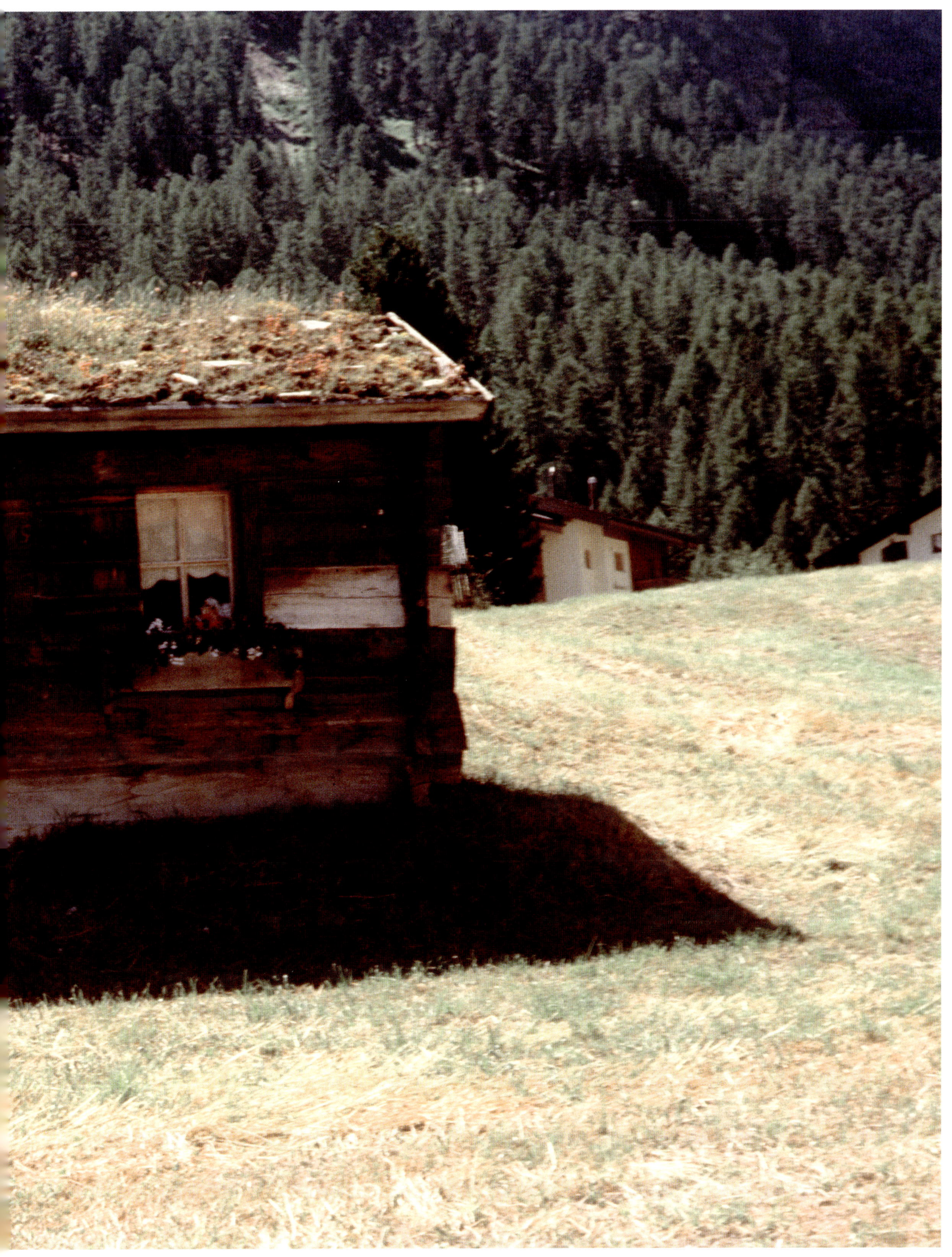

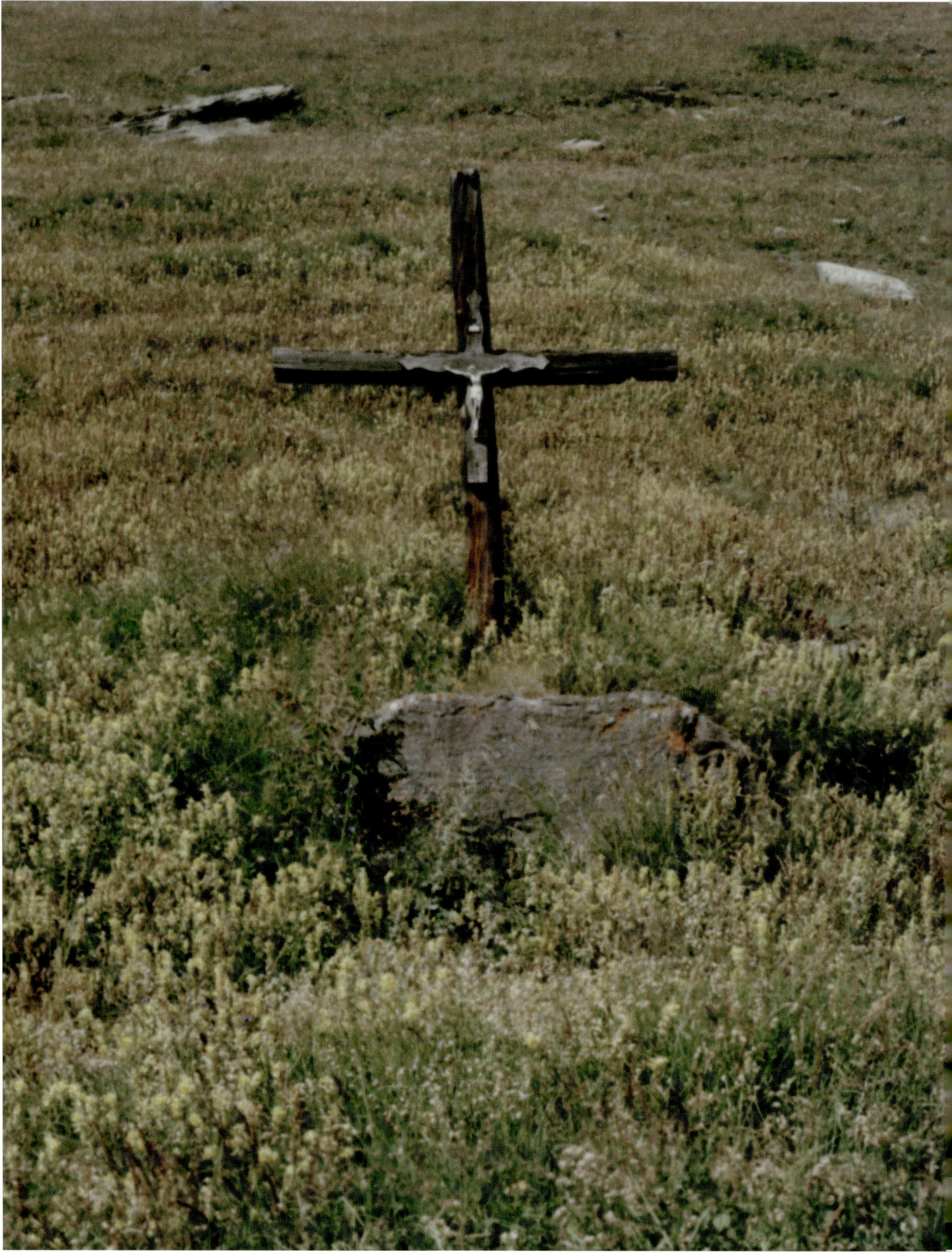

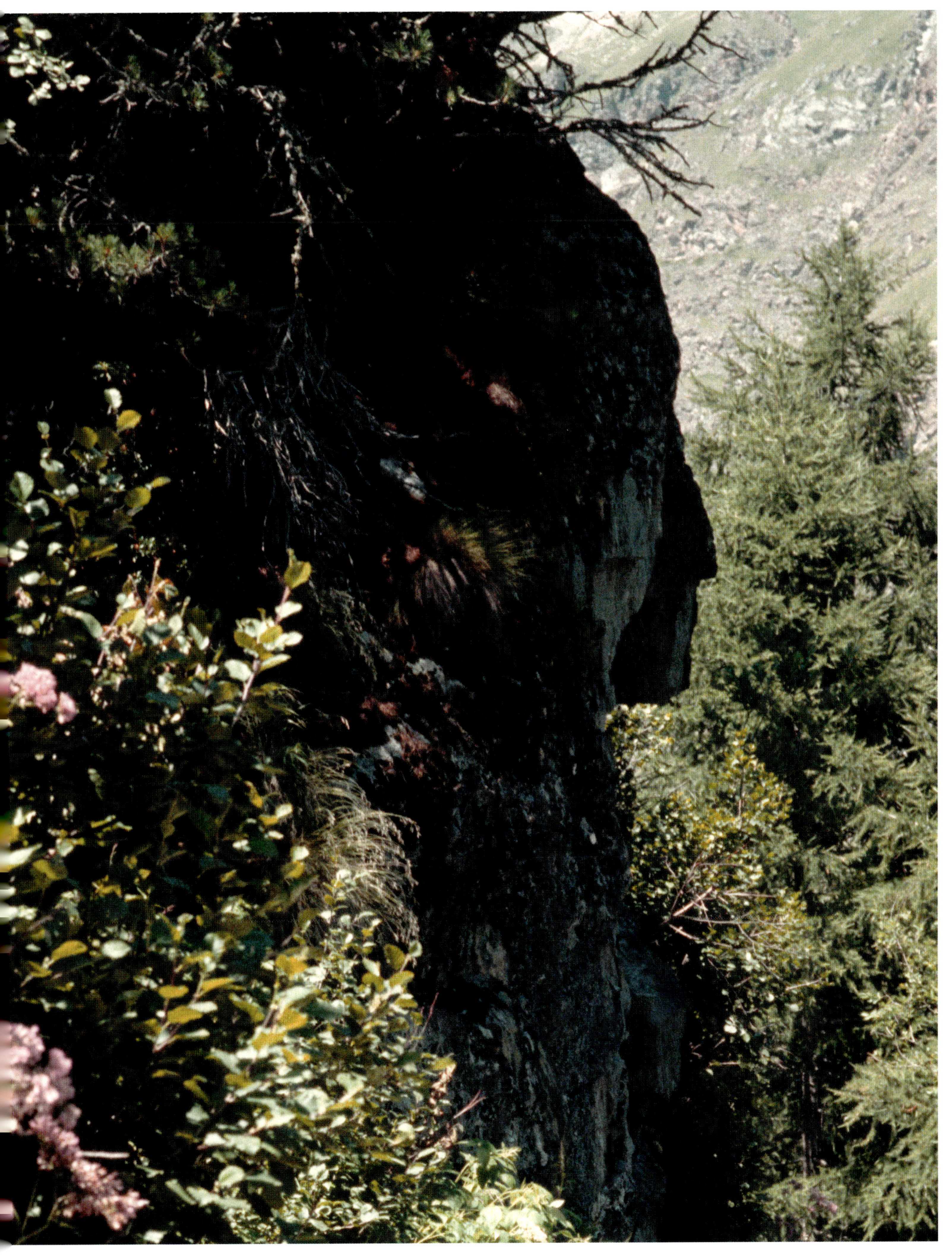

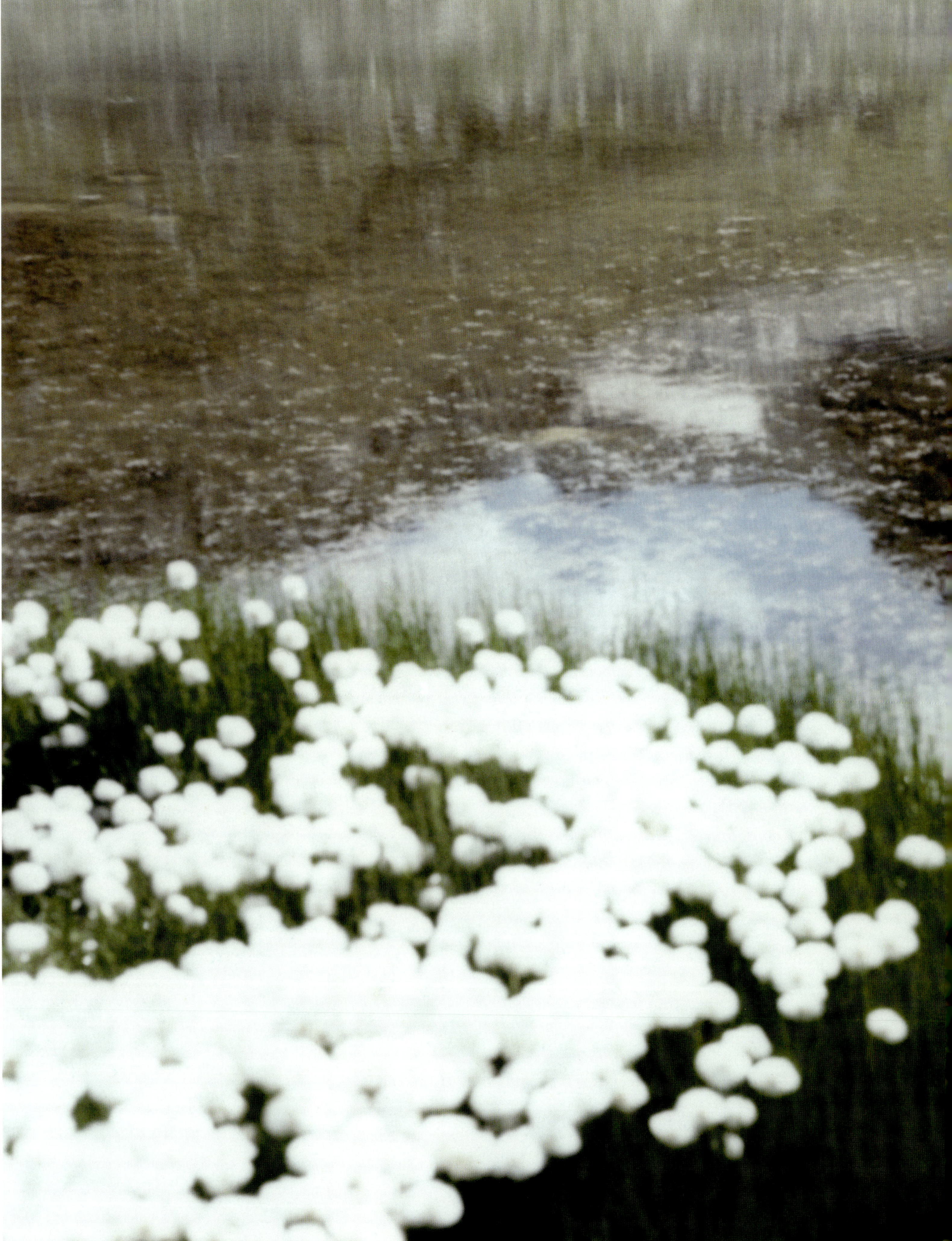

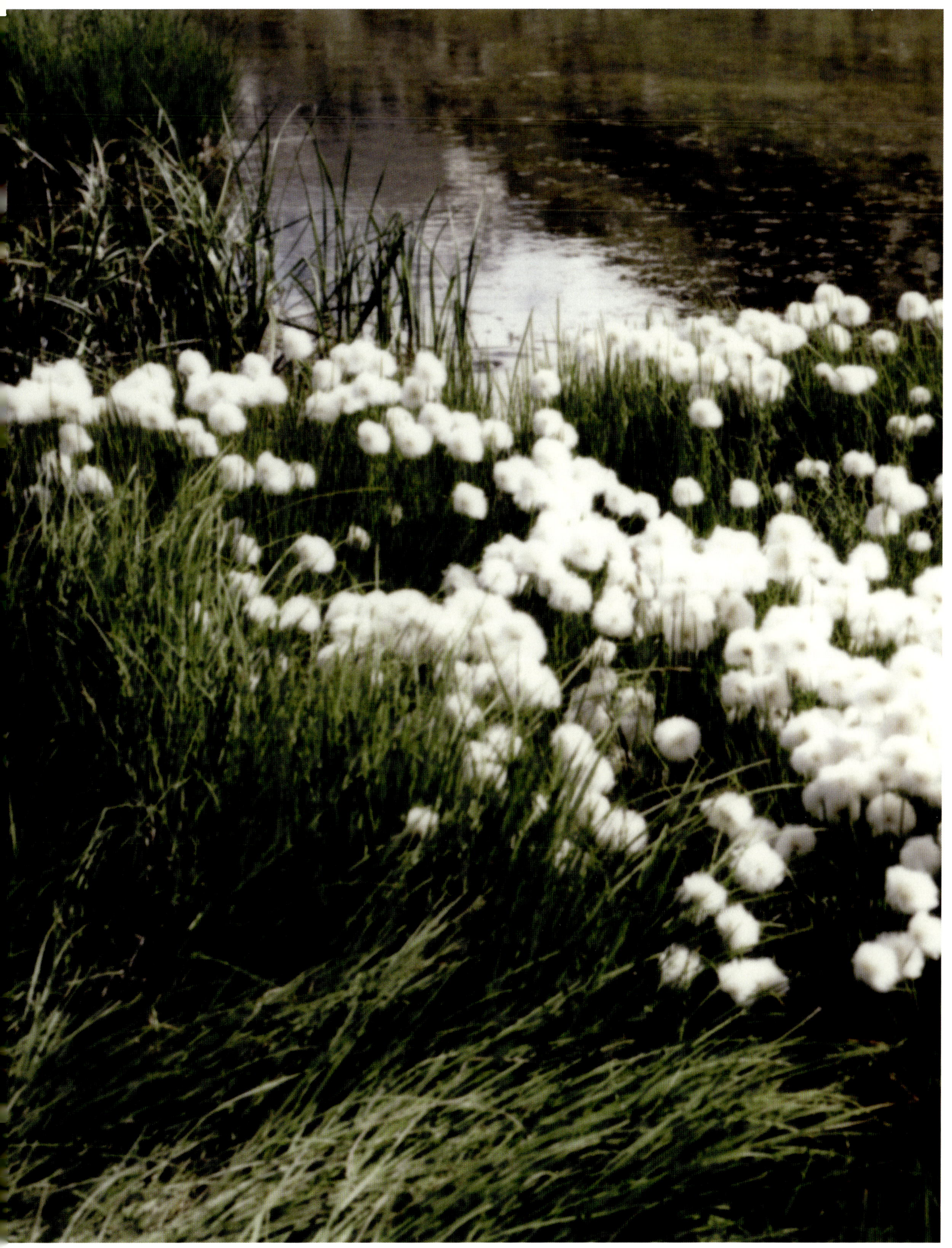

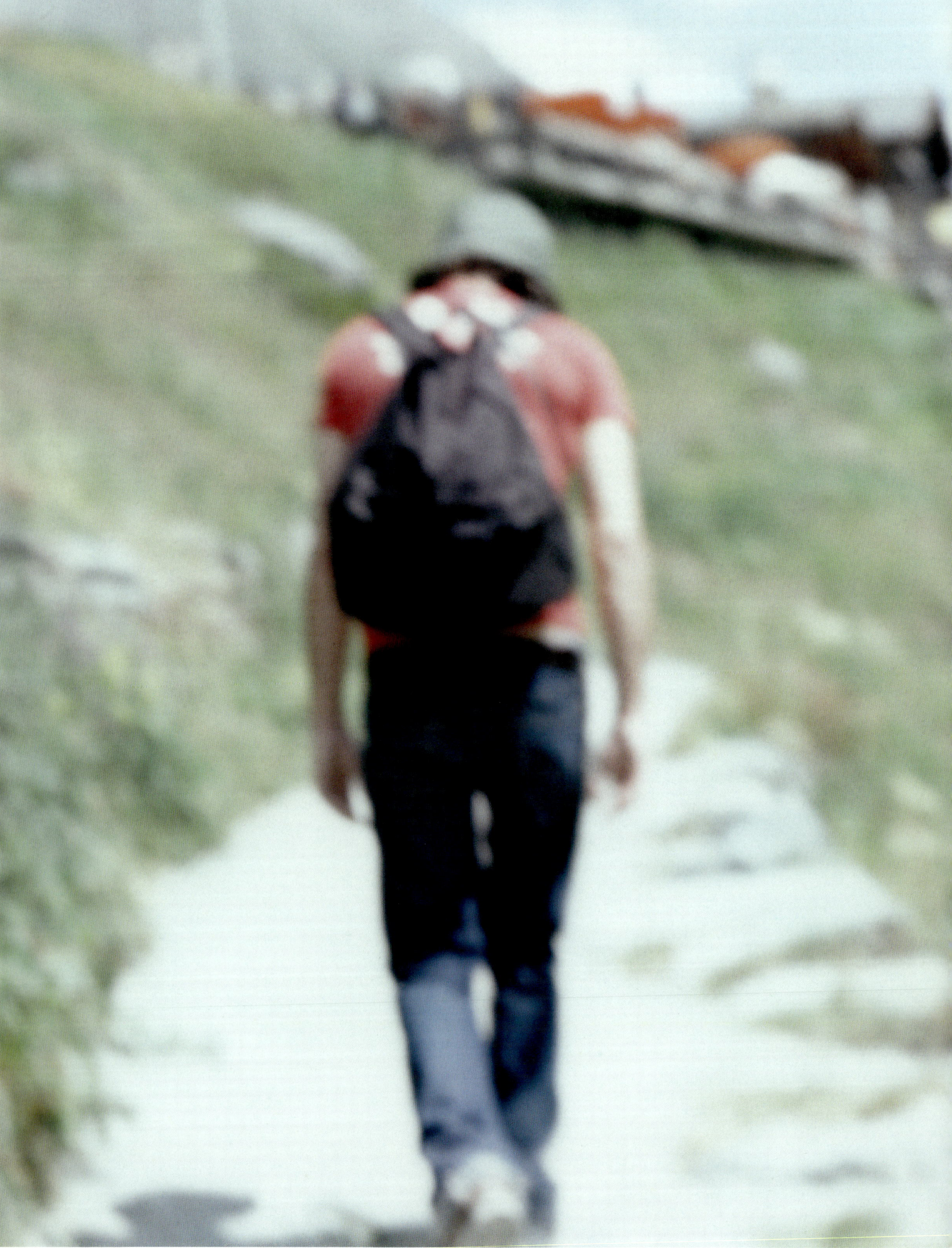

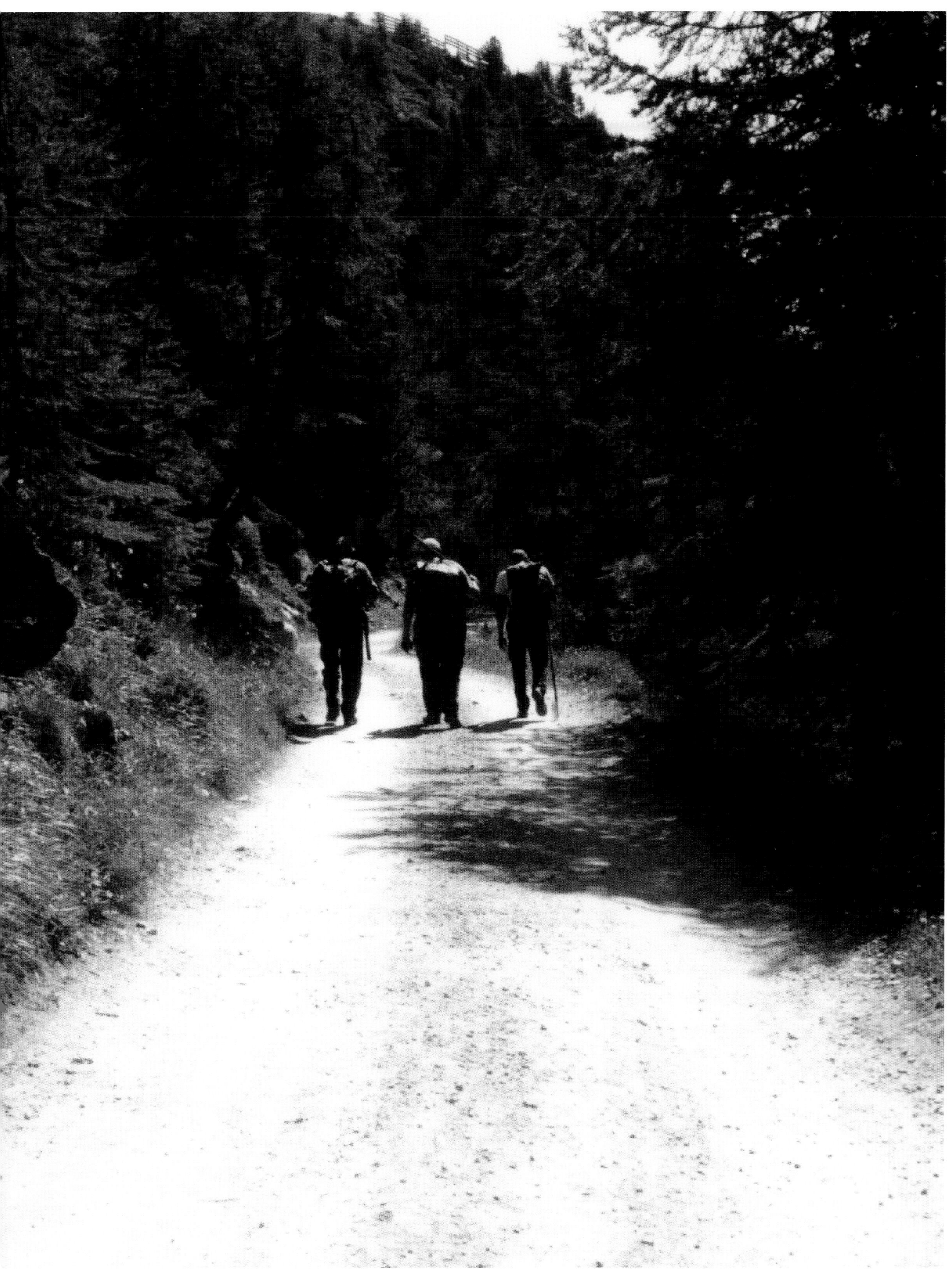

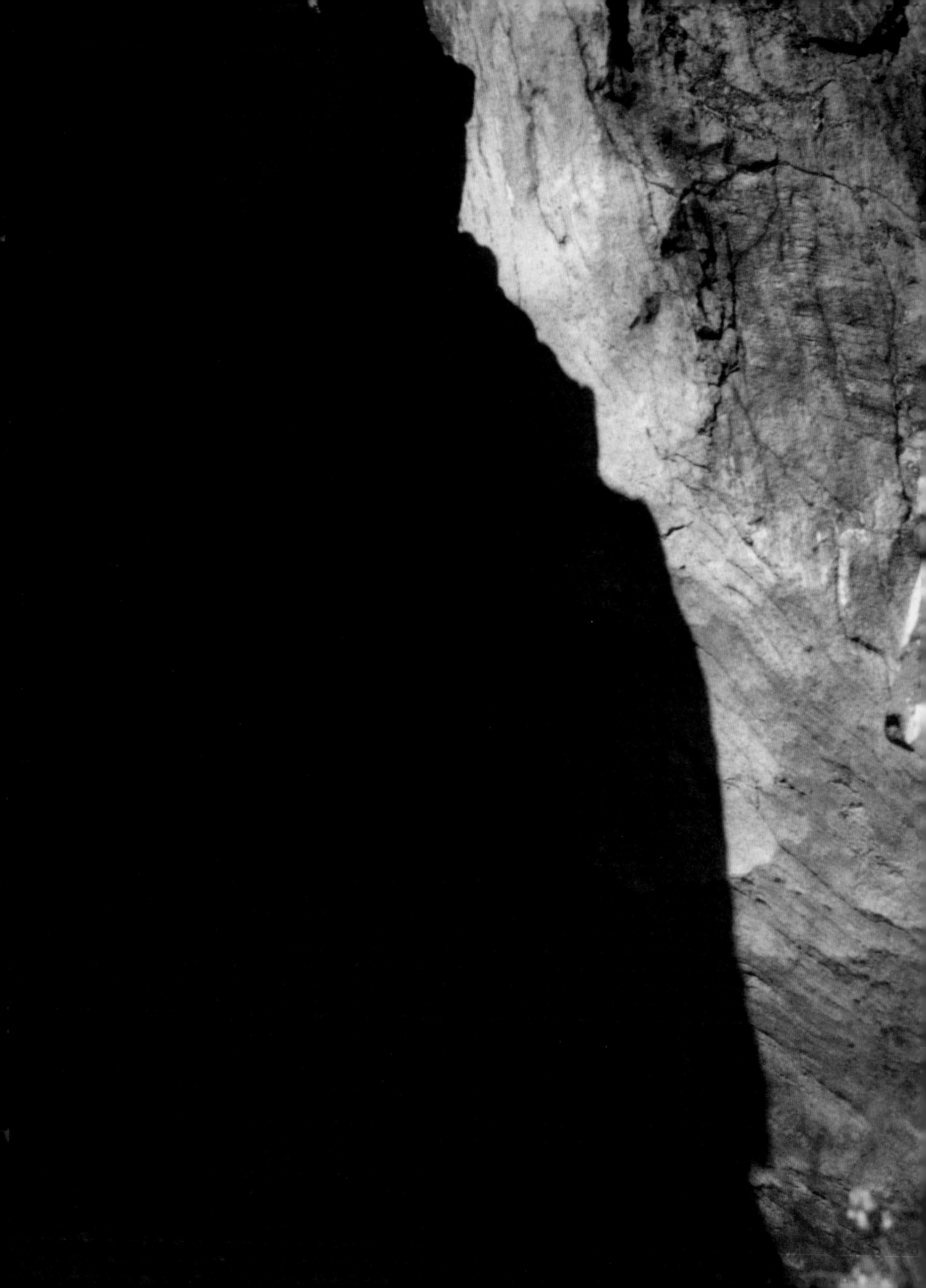

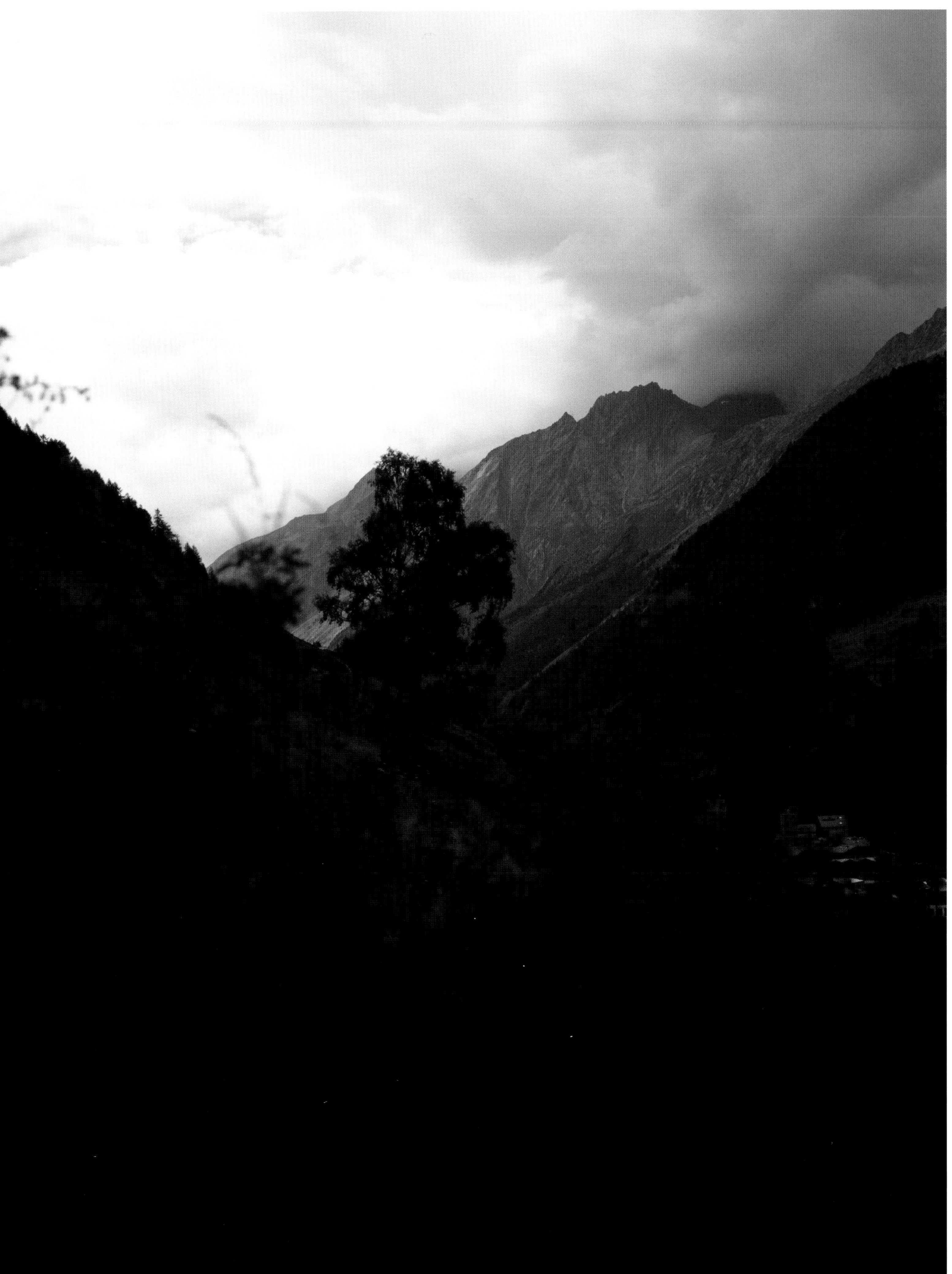

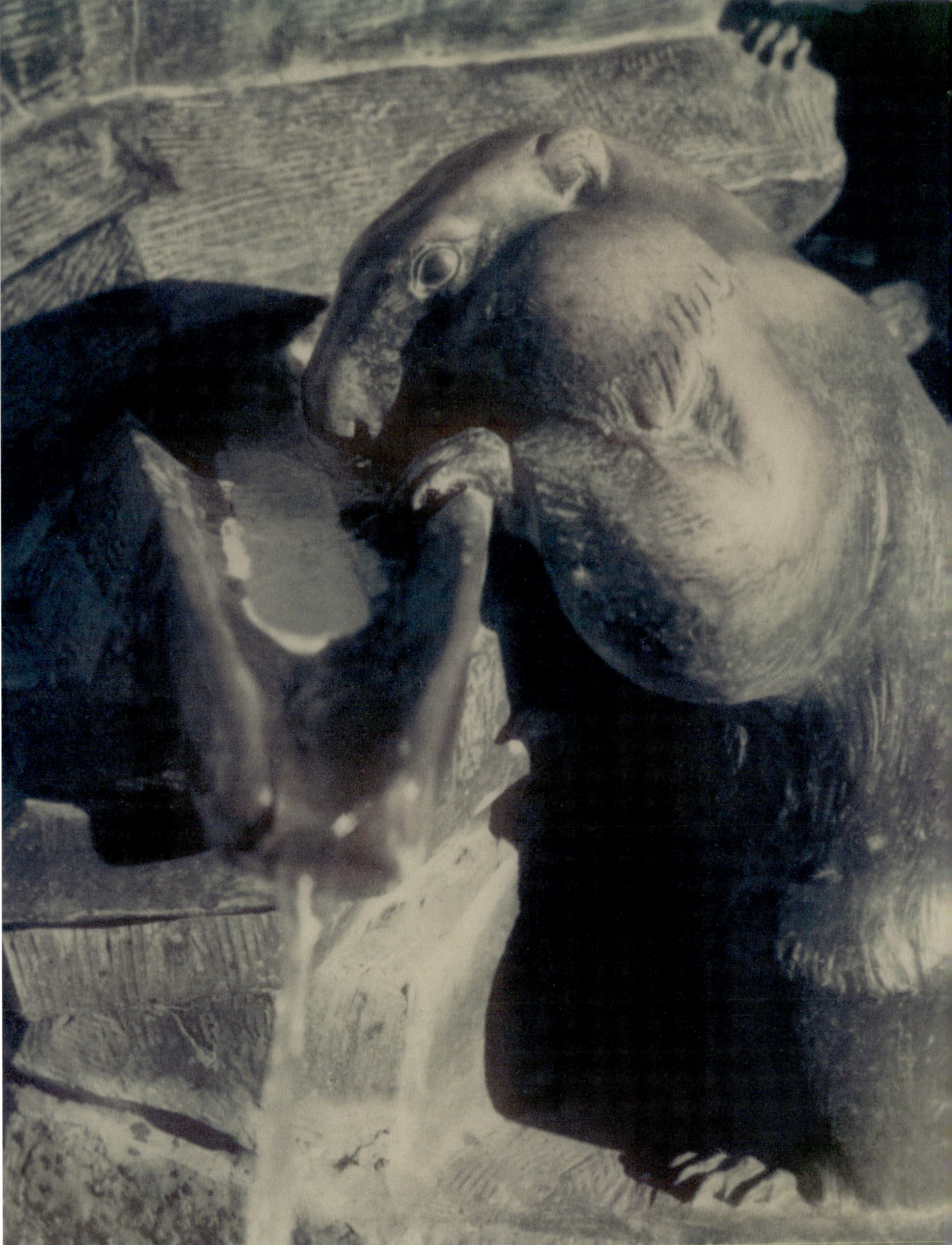

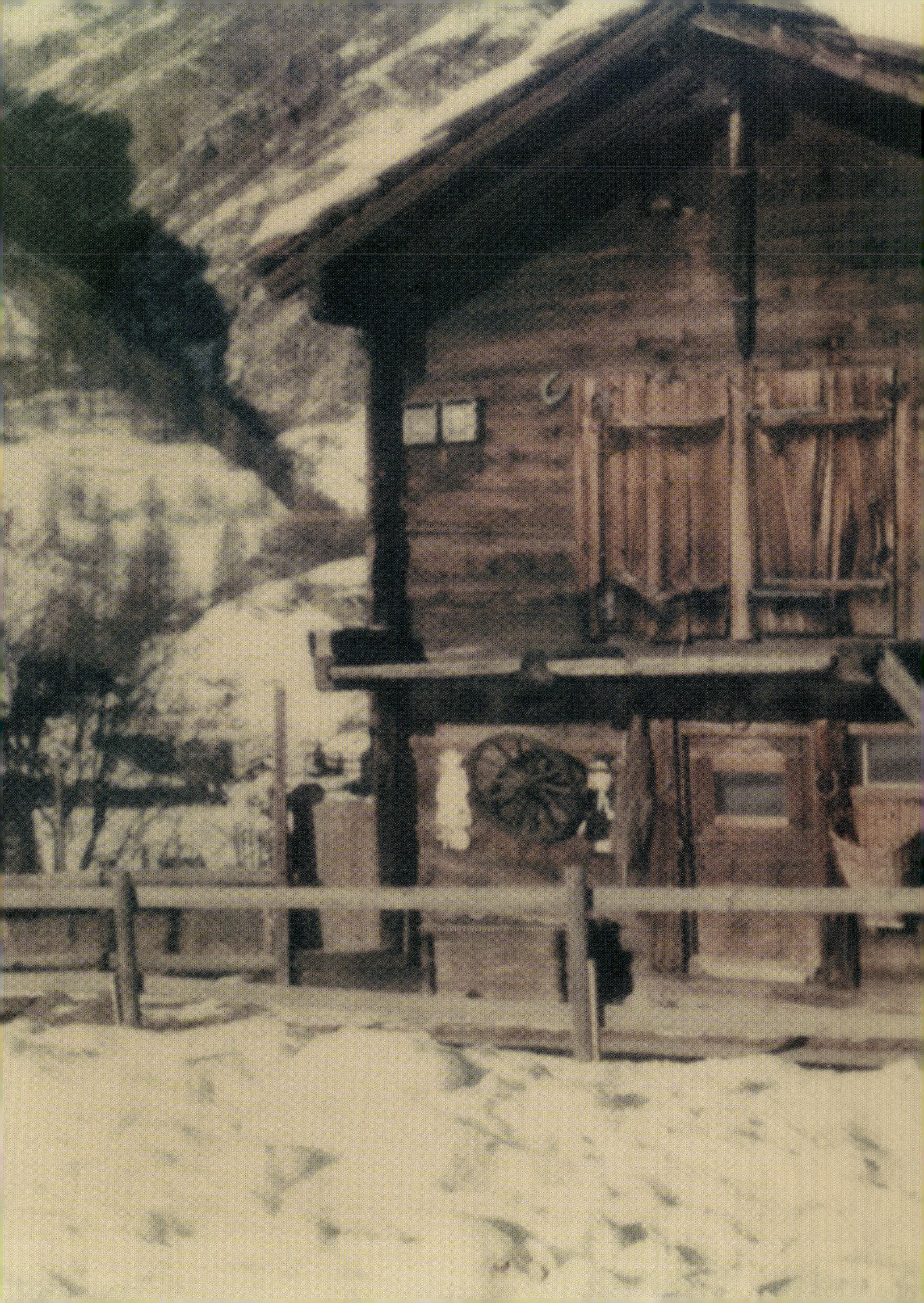

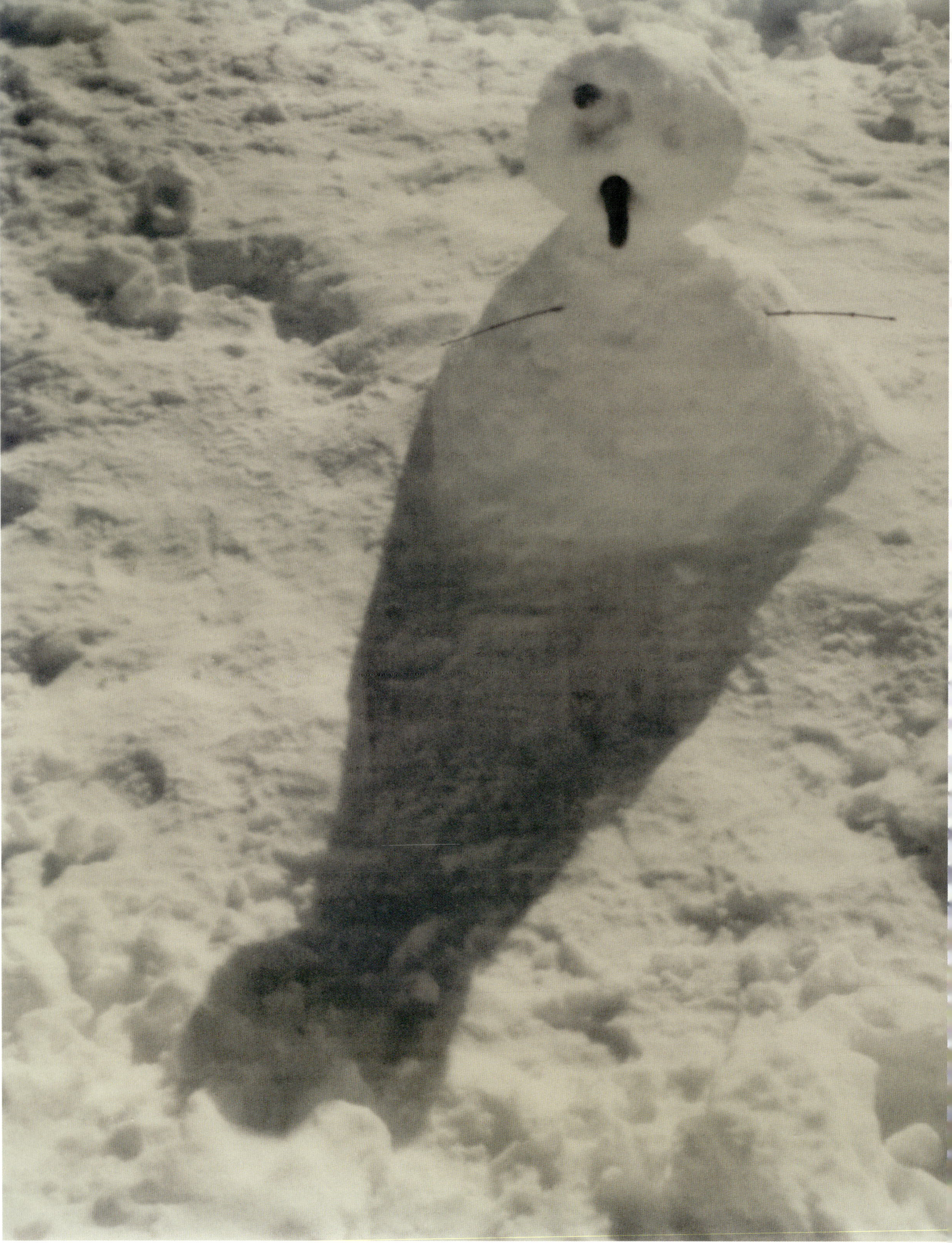

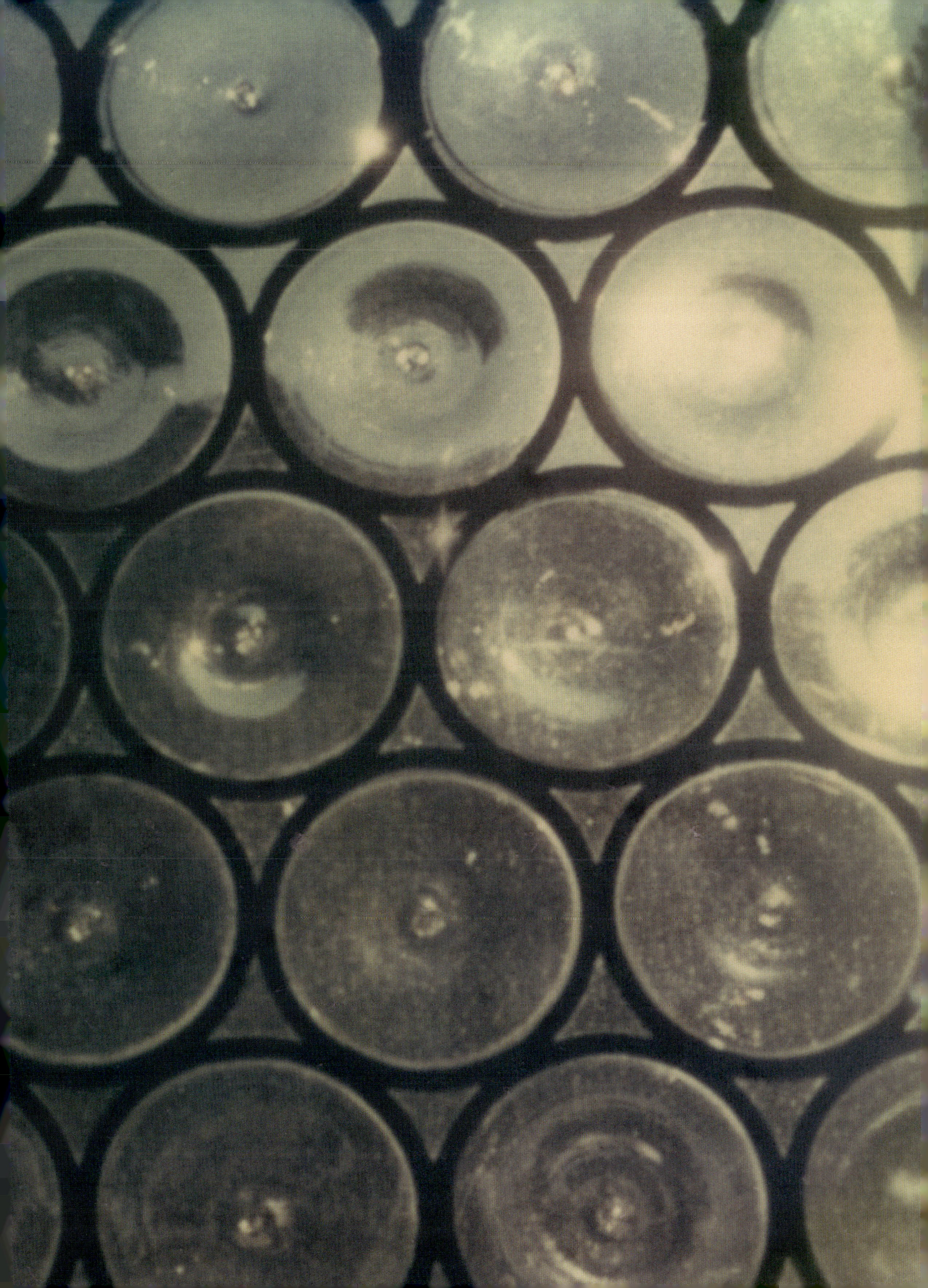

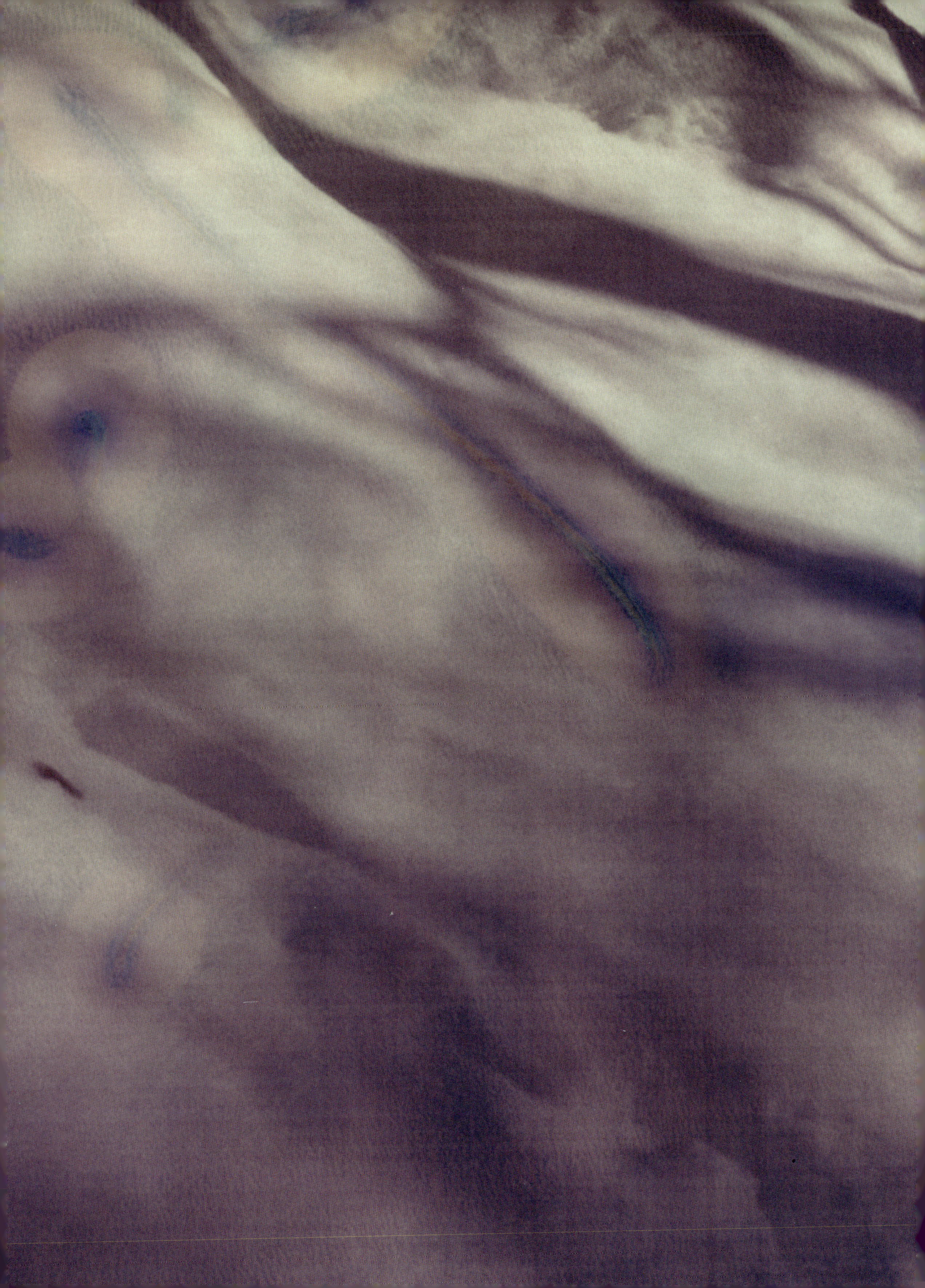

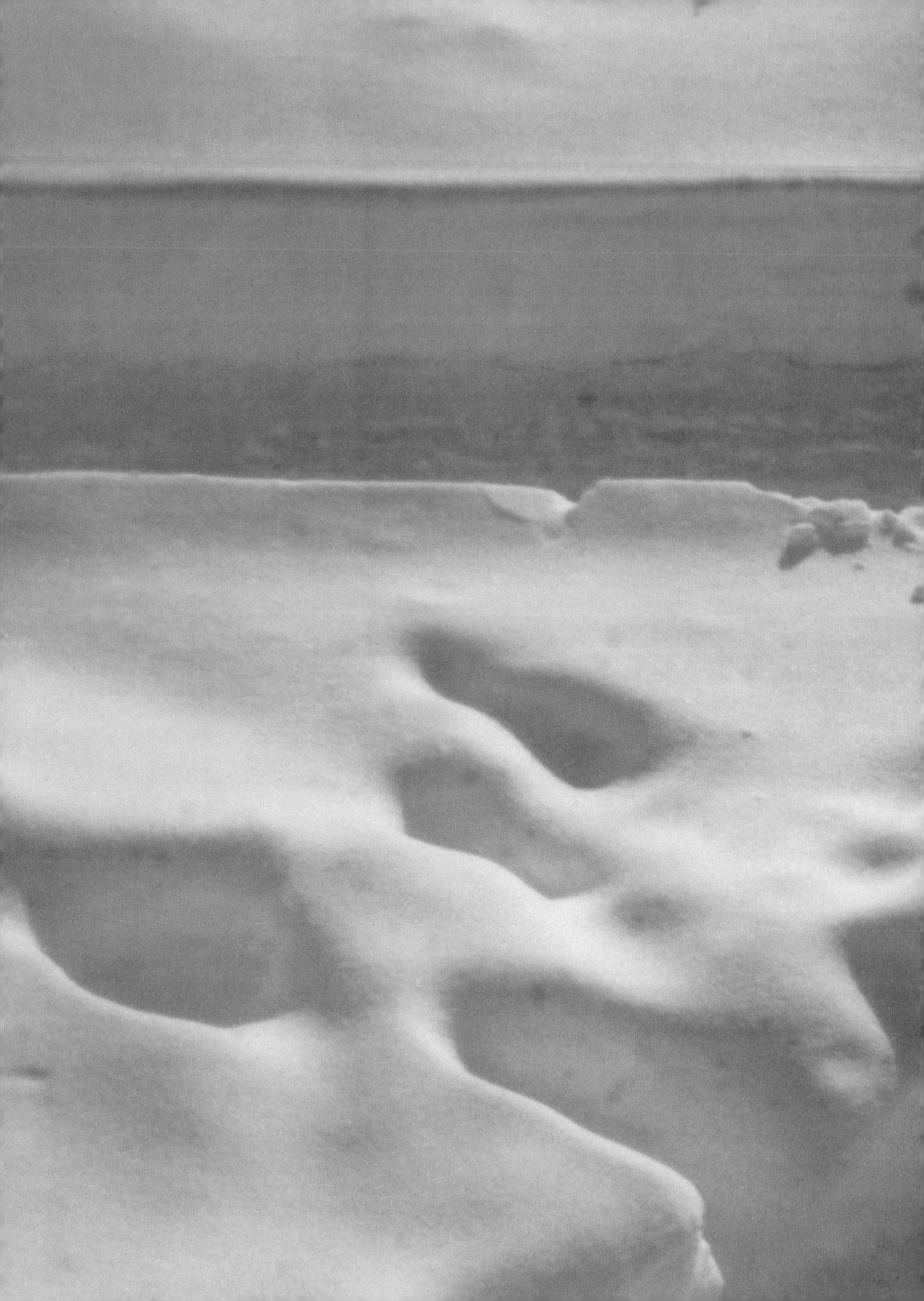

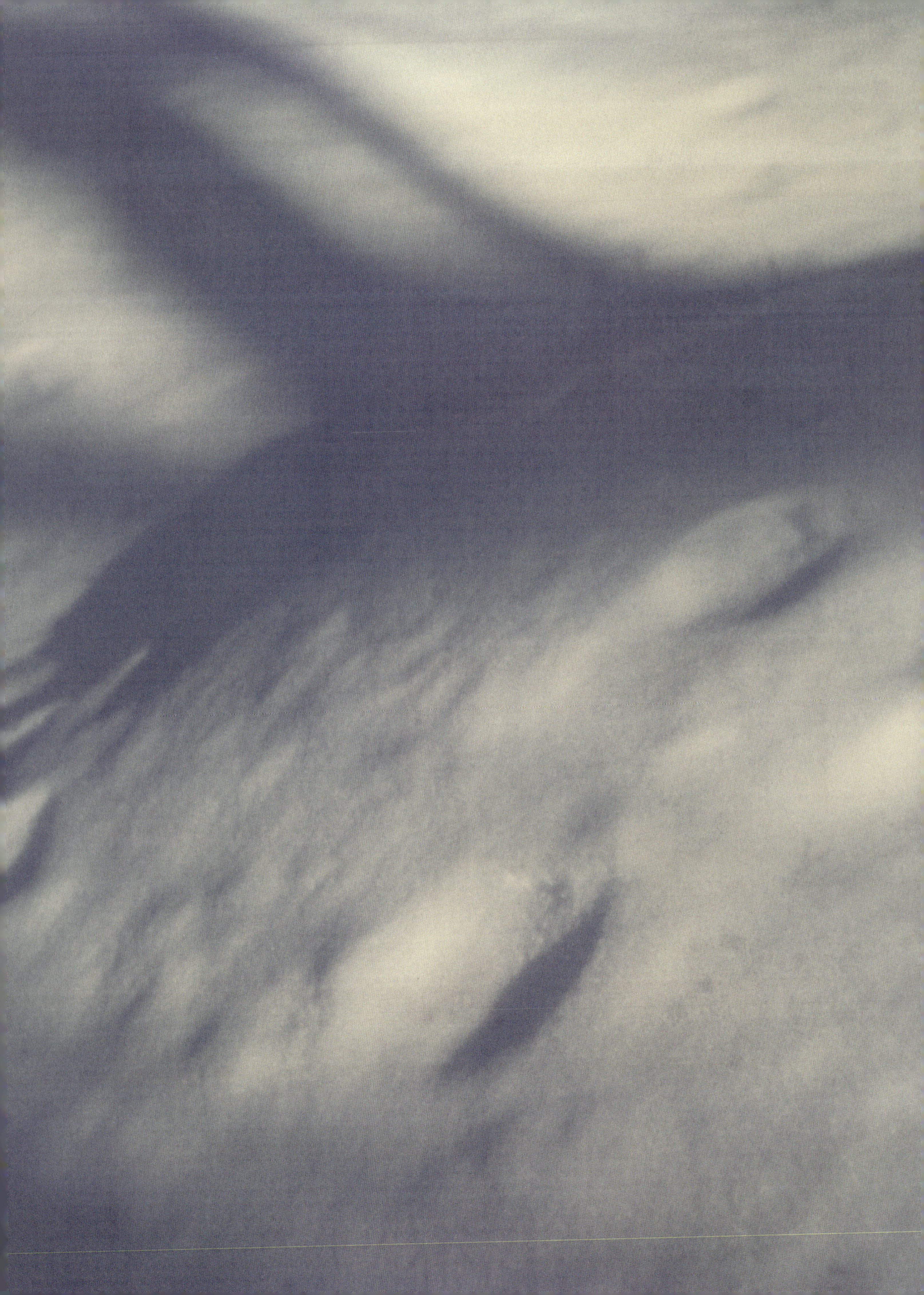

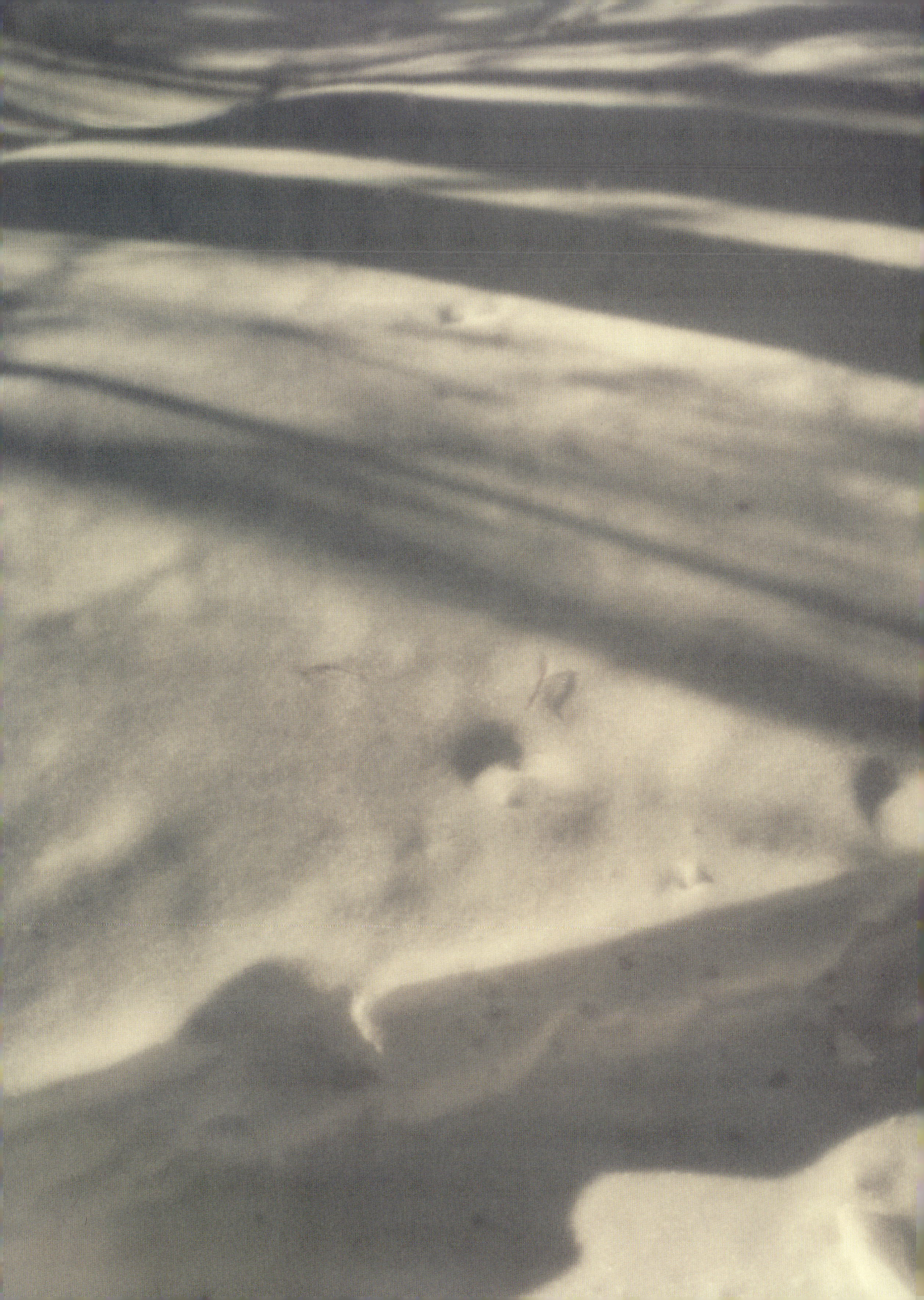

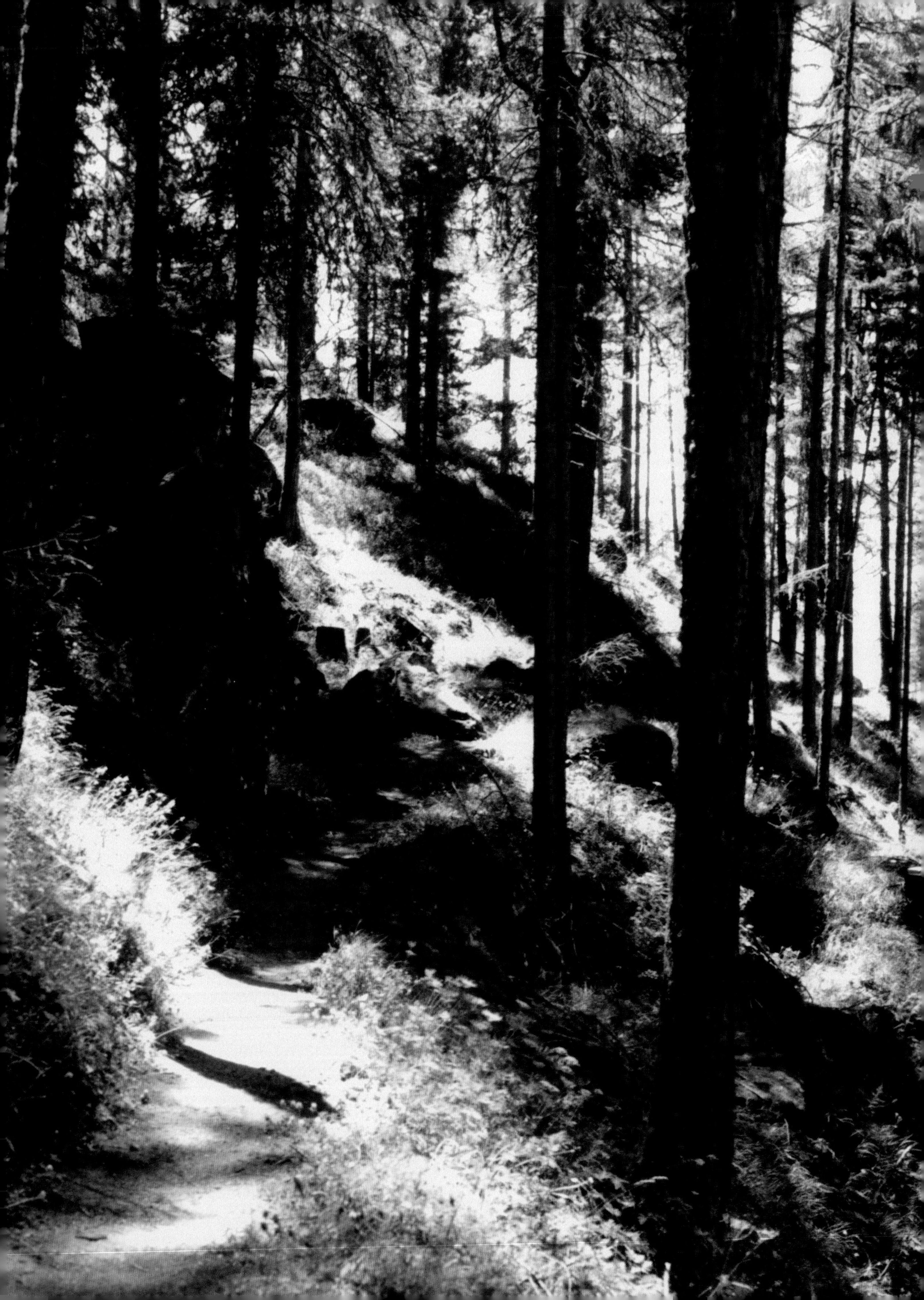

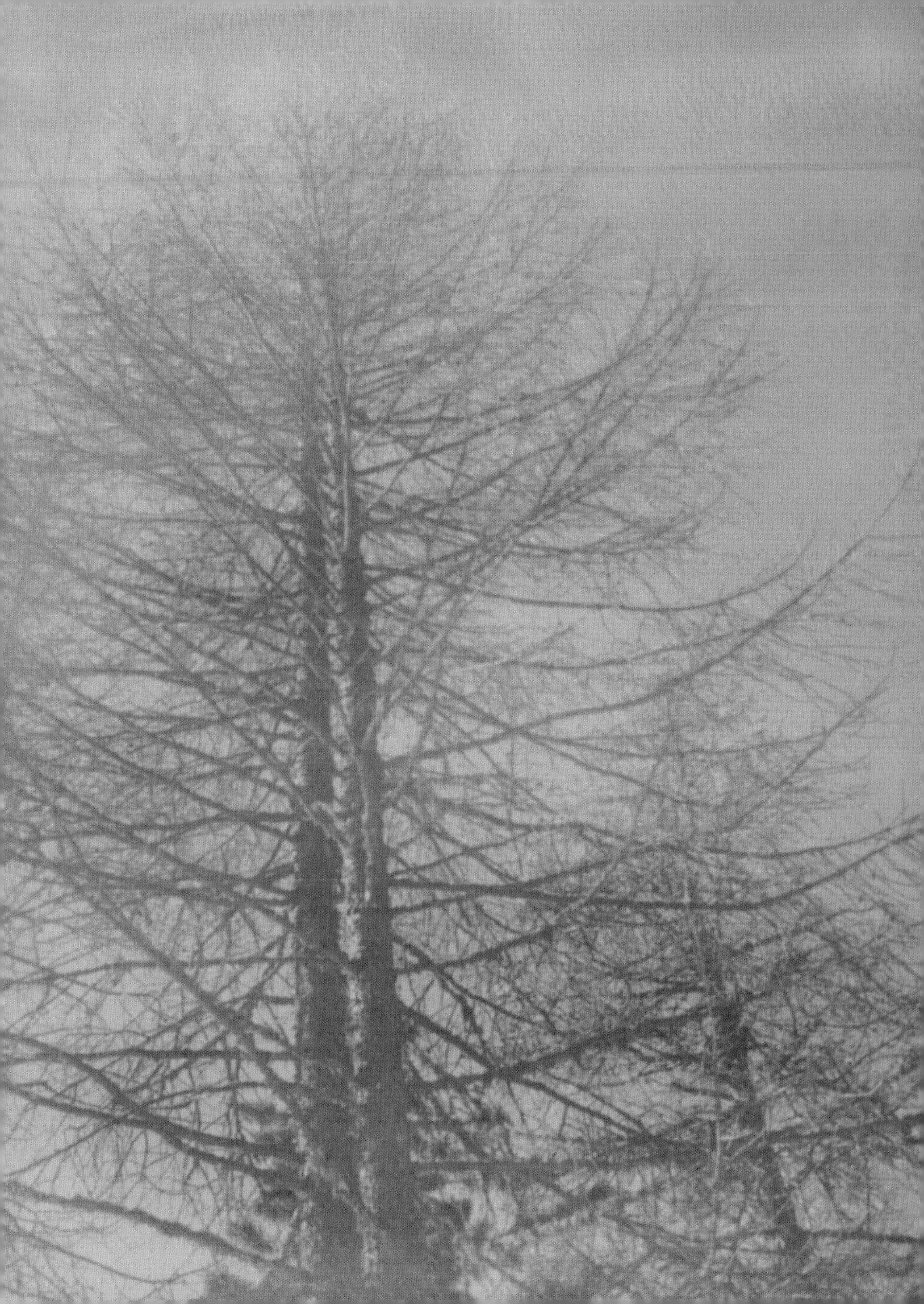

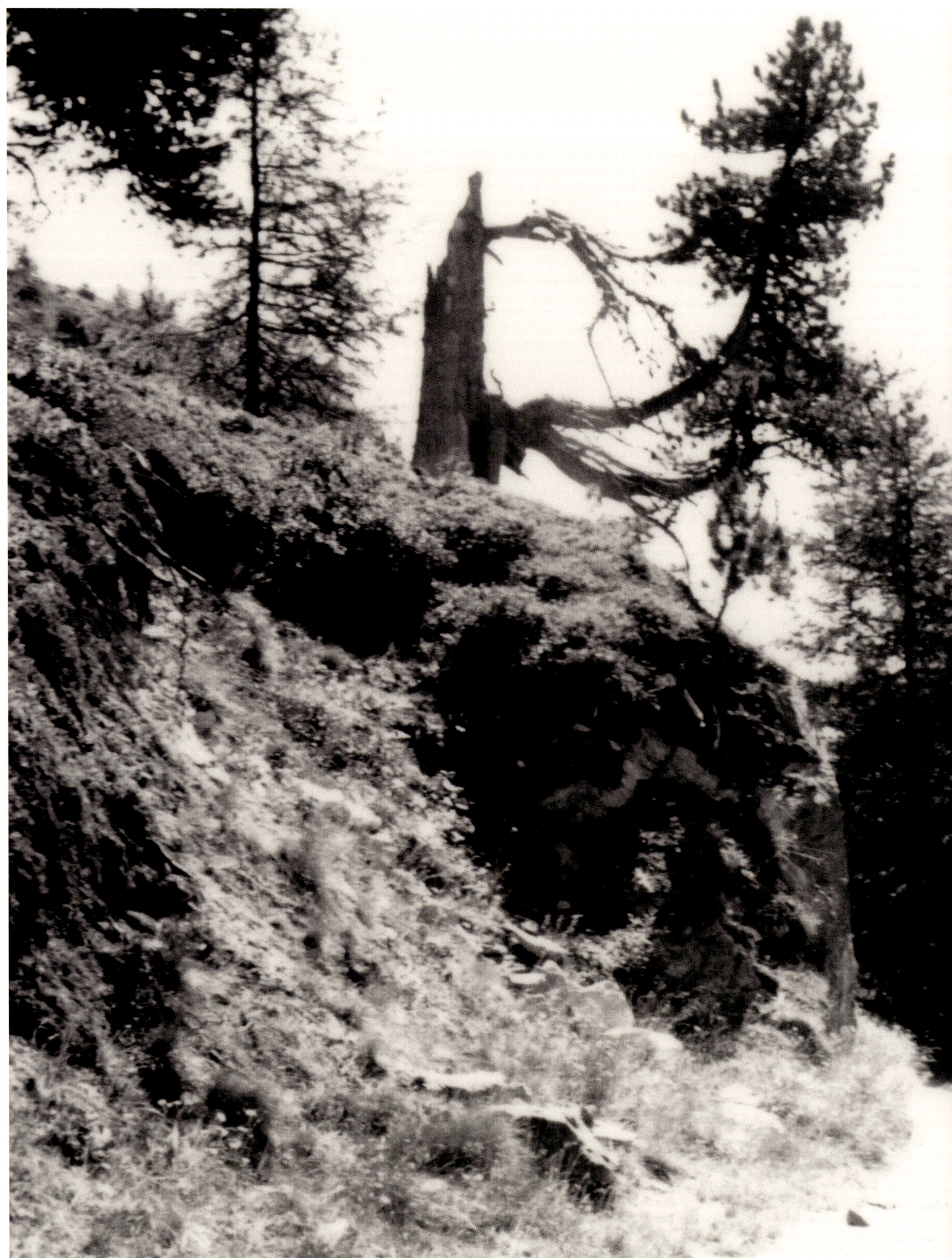

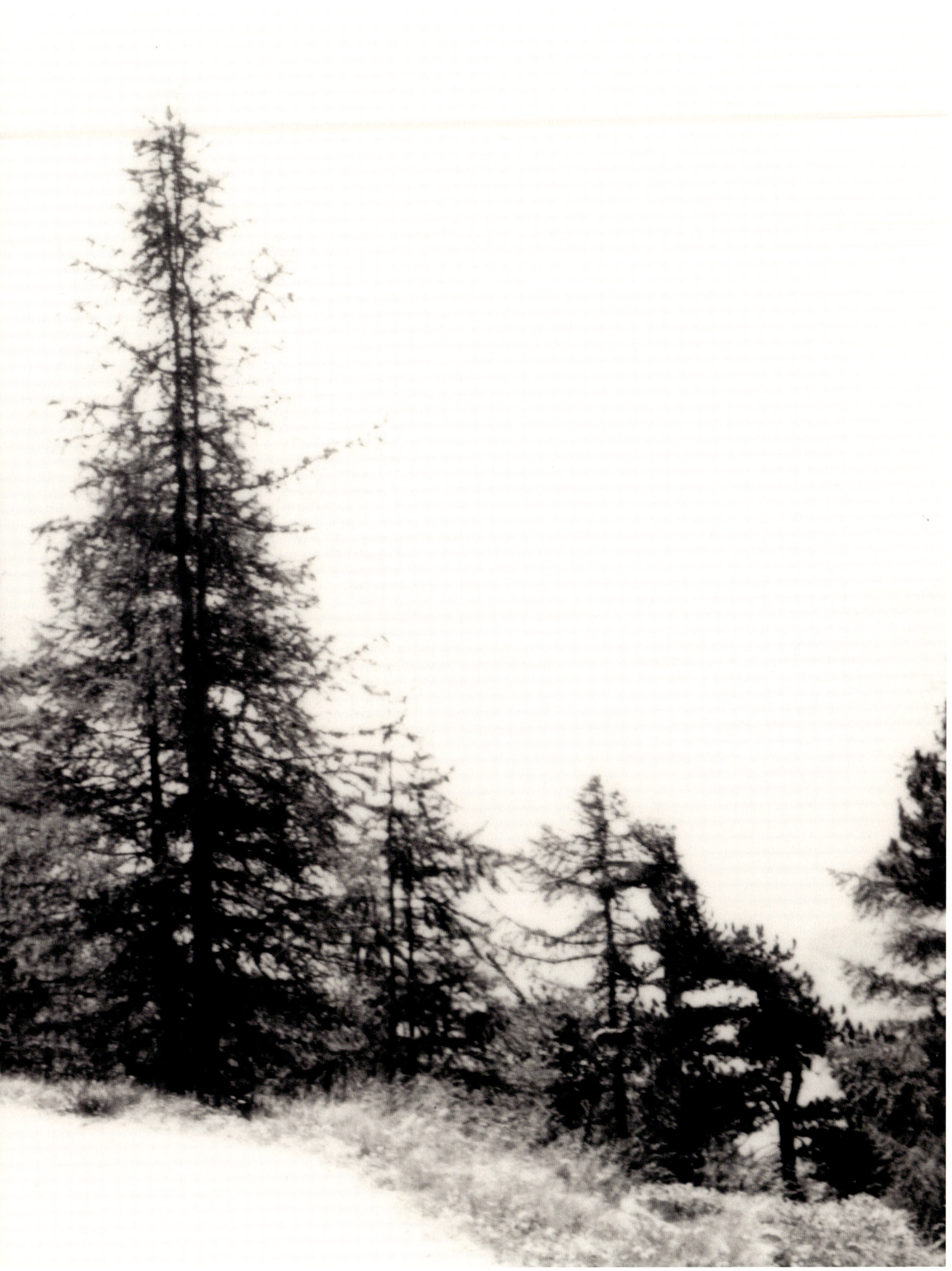

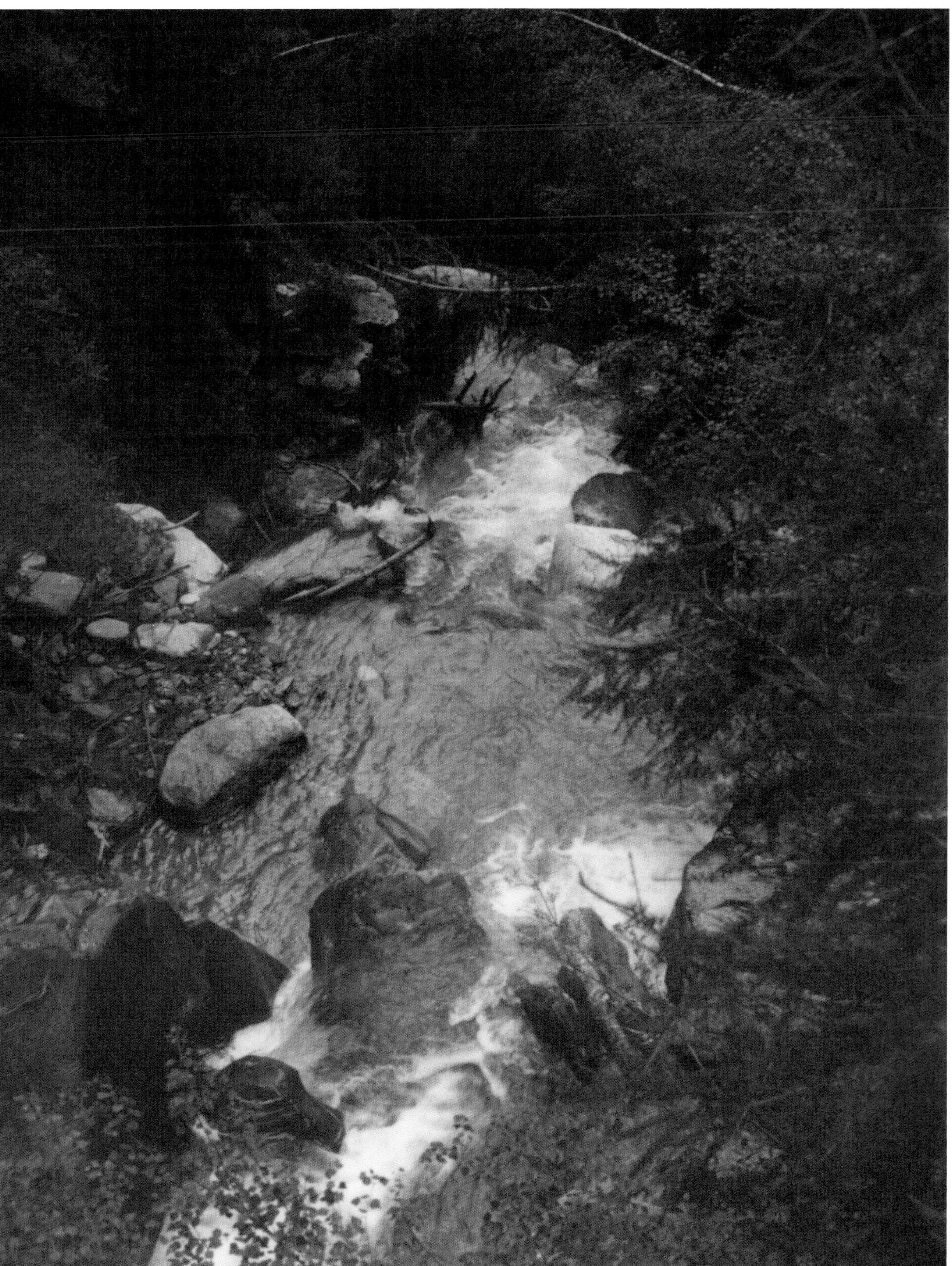

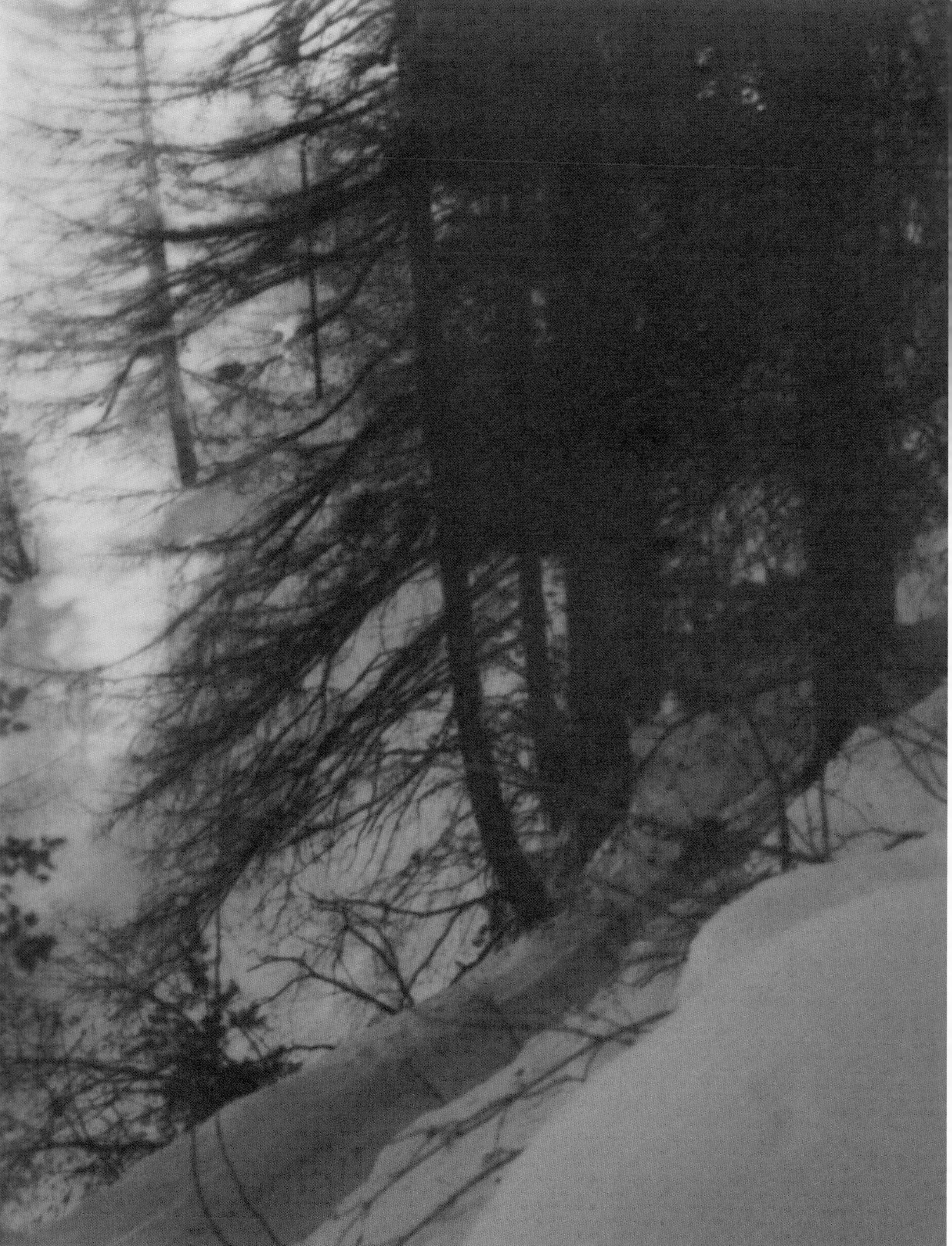

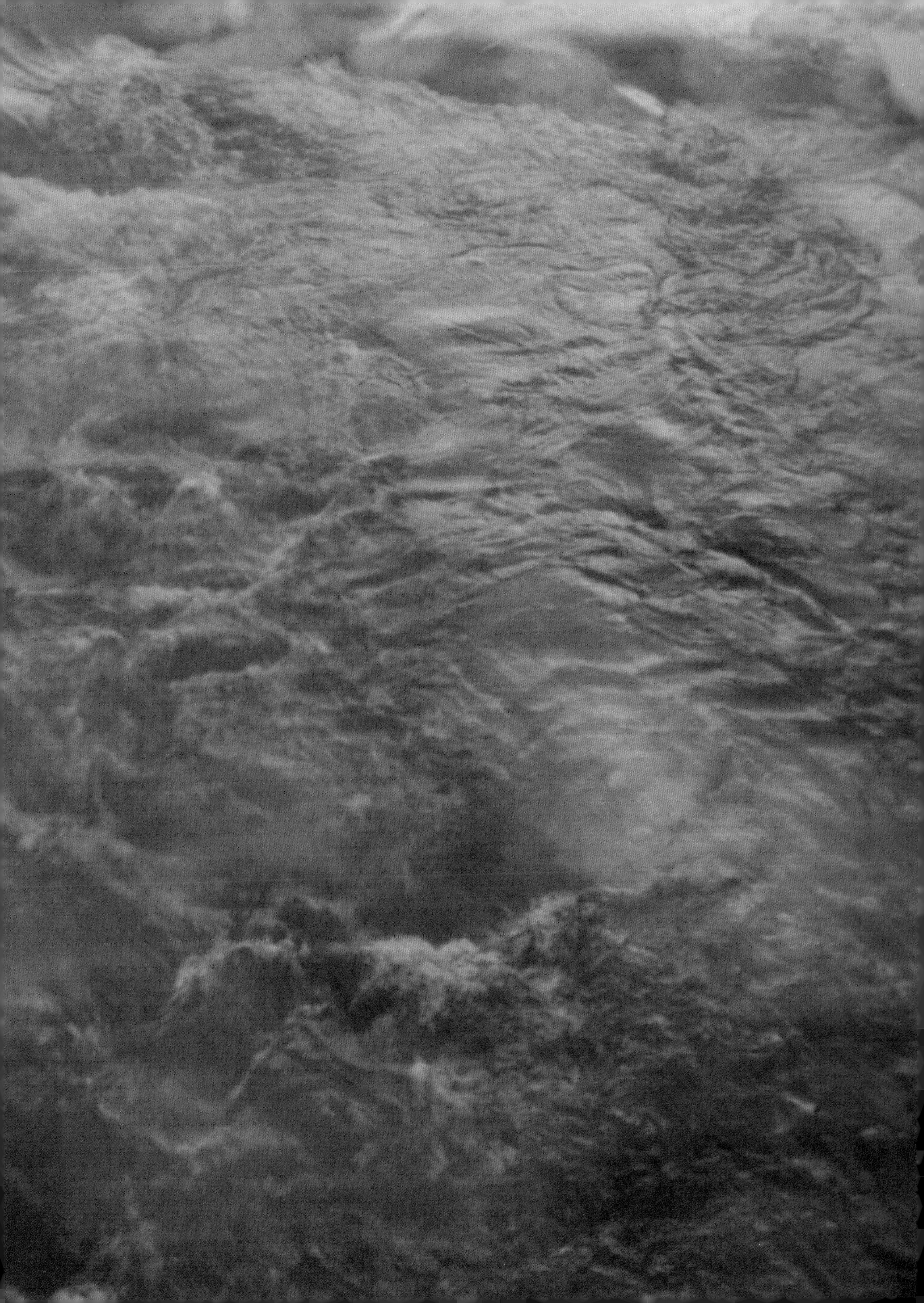

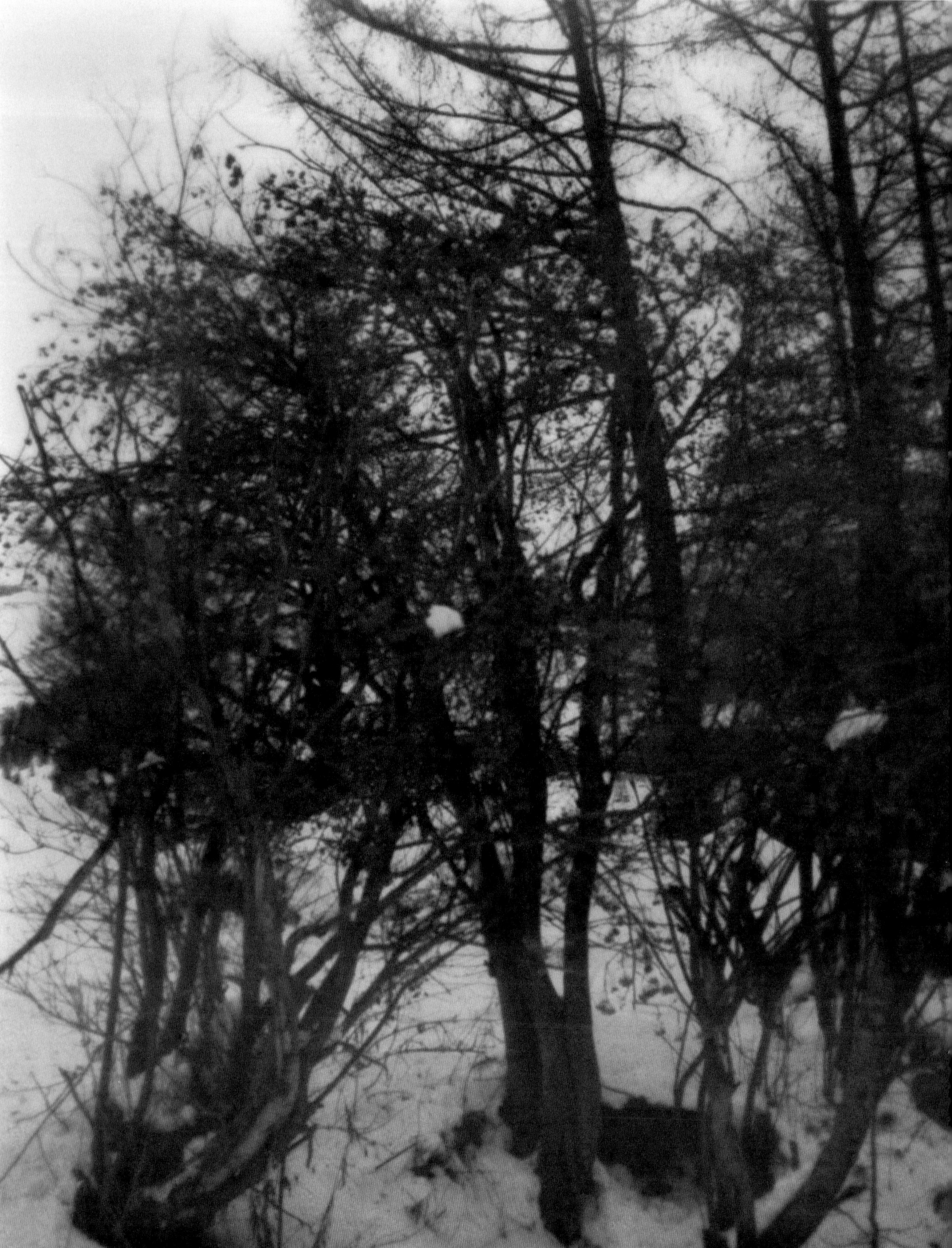

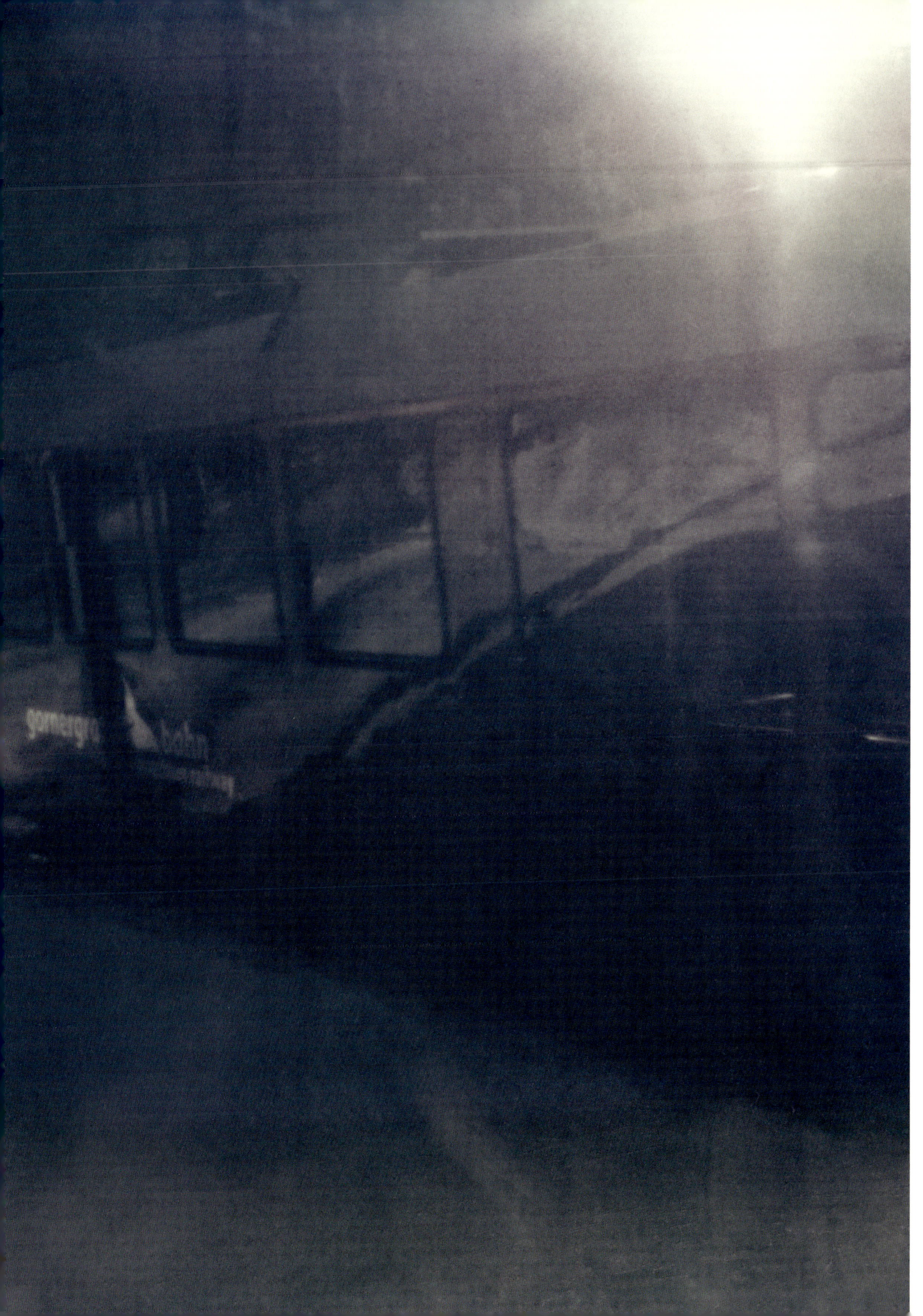
gornergrat bahn

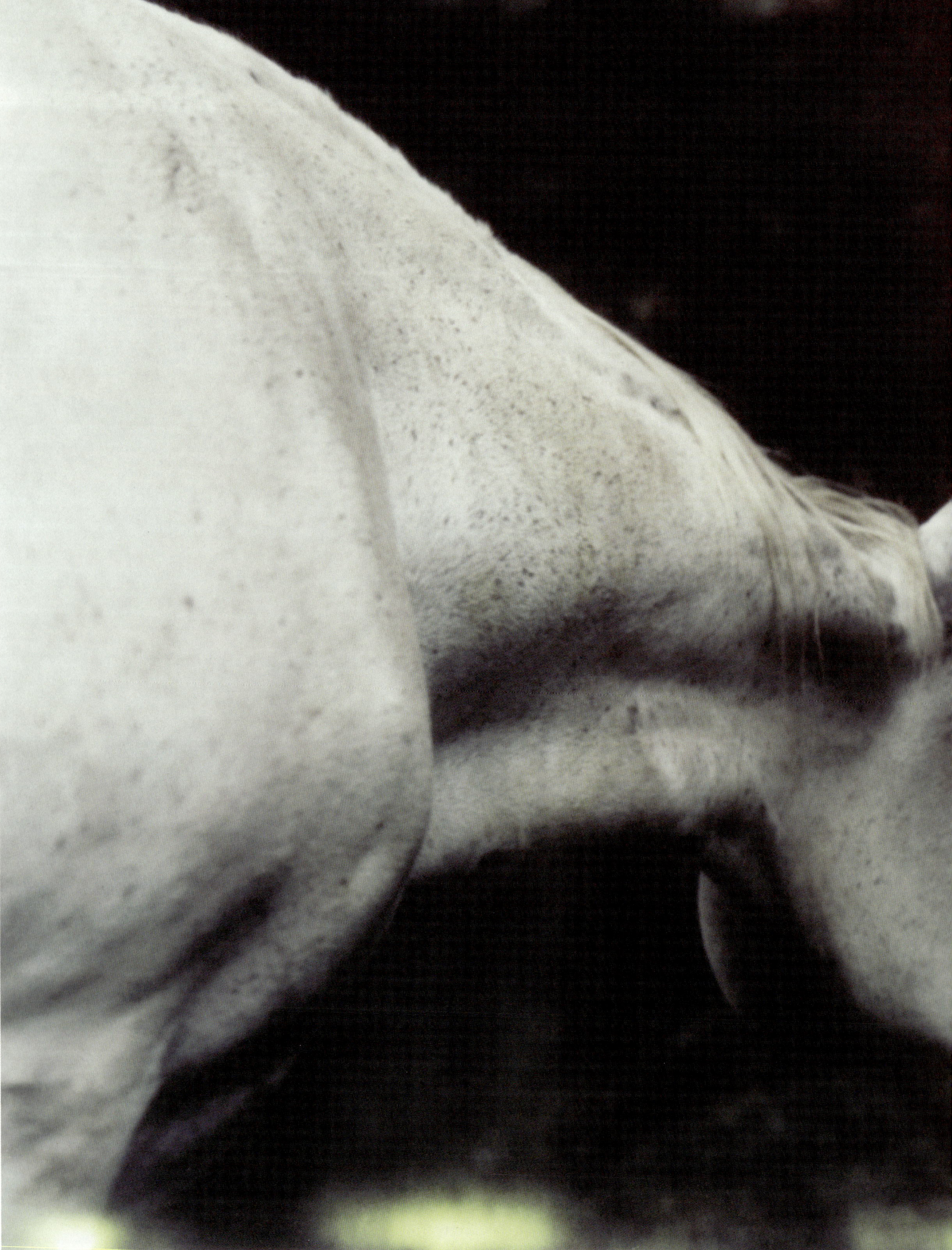

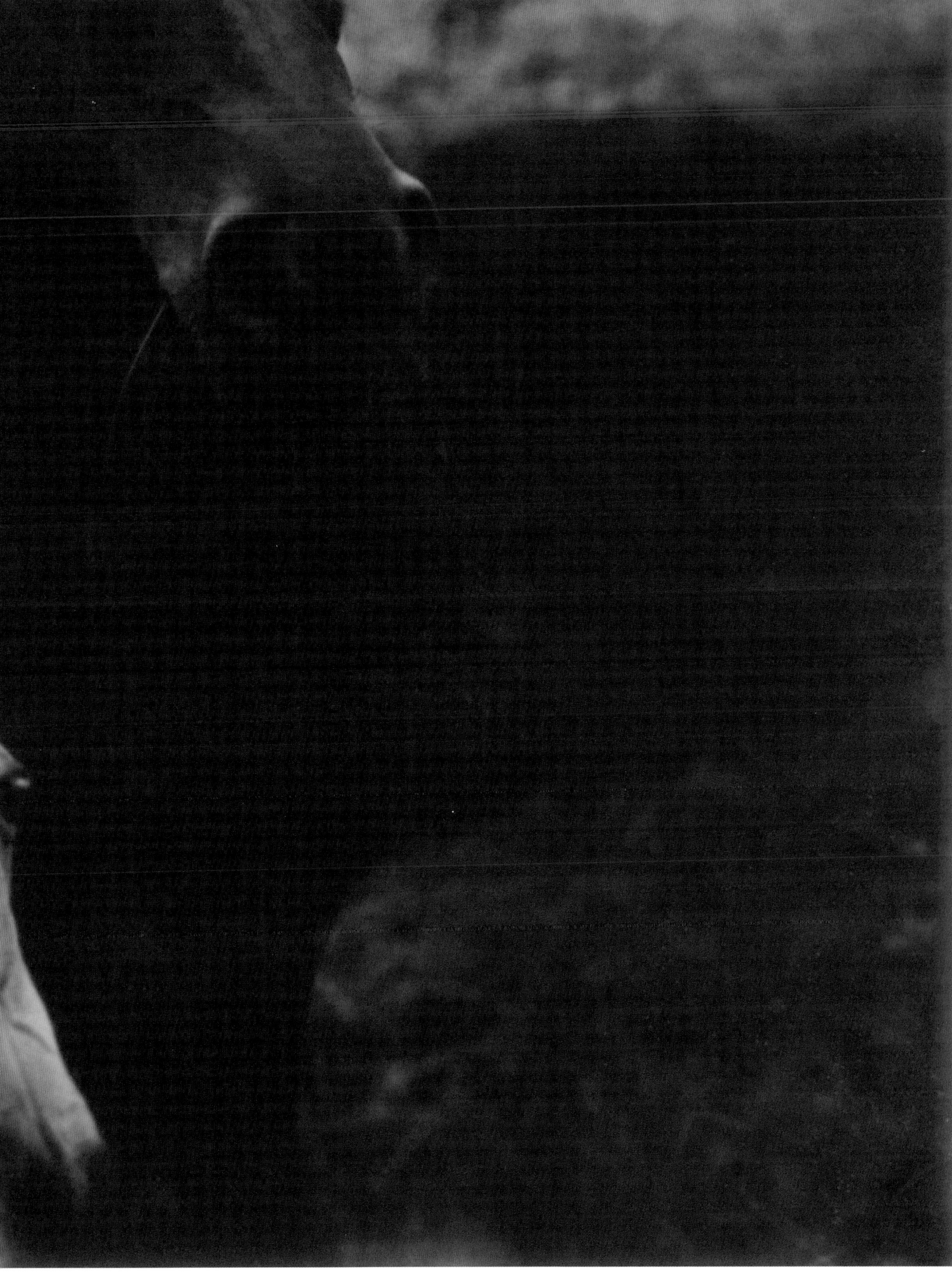

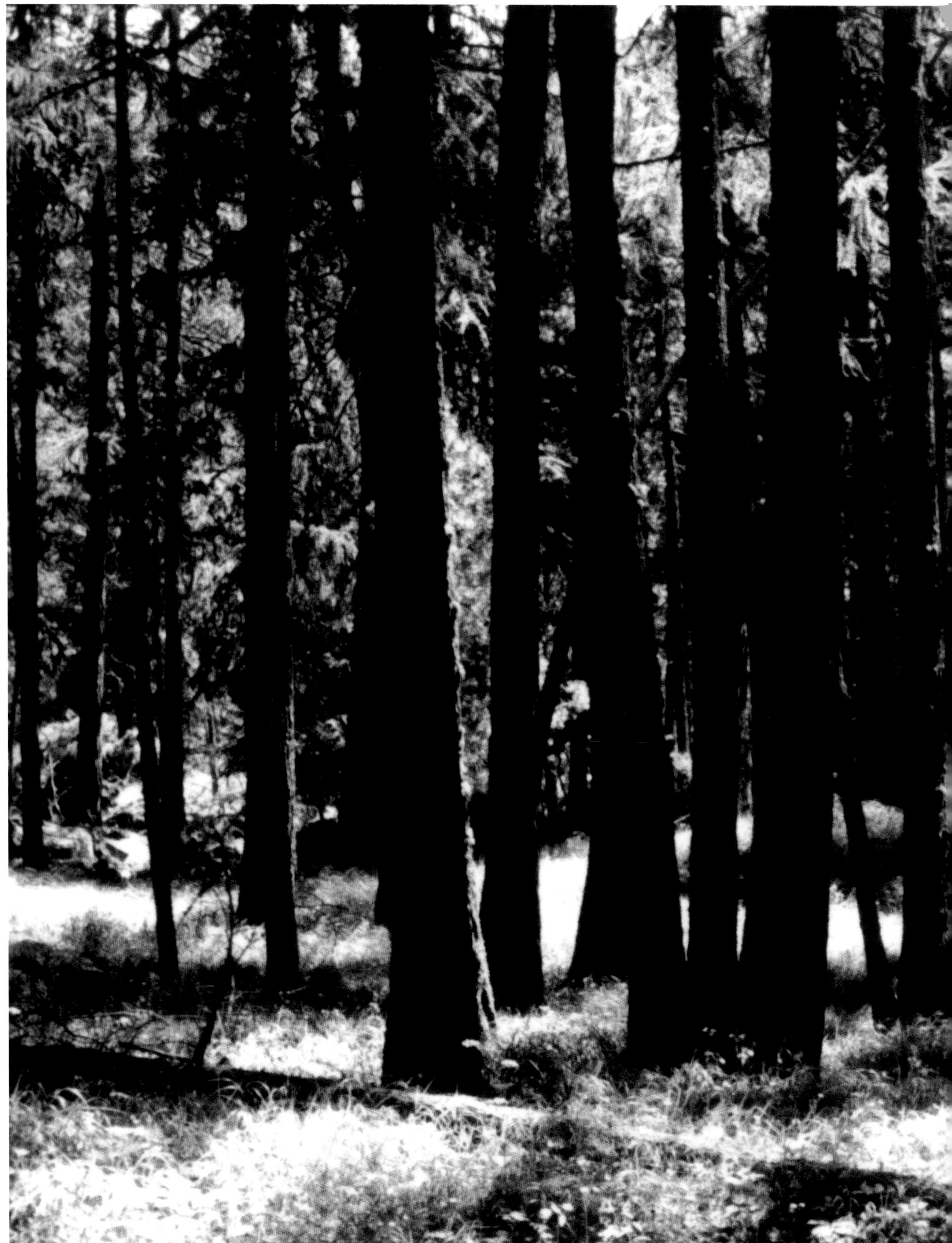

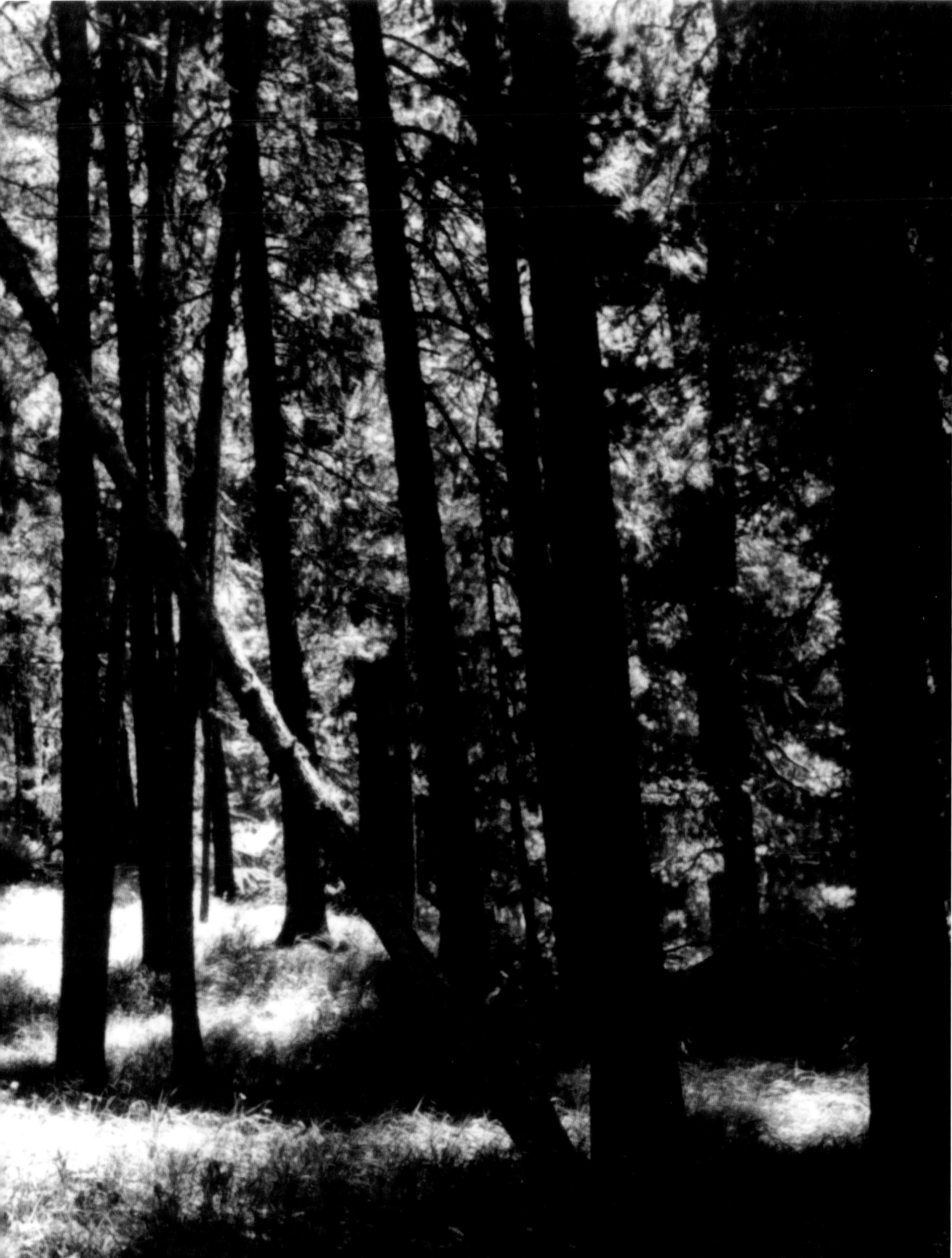

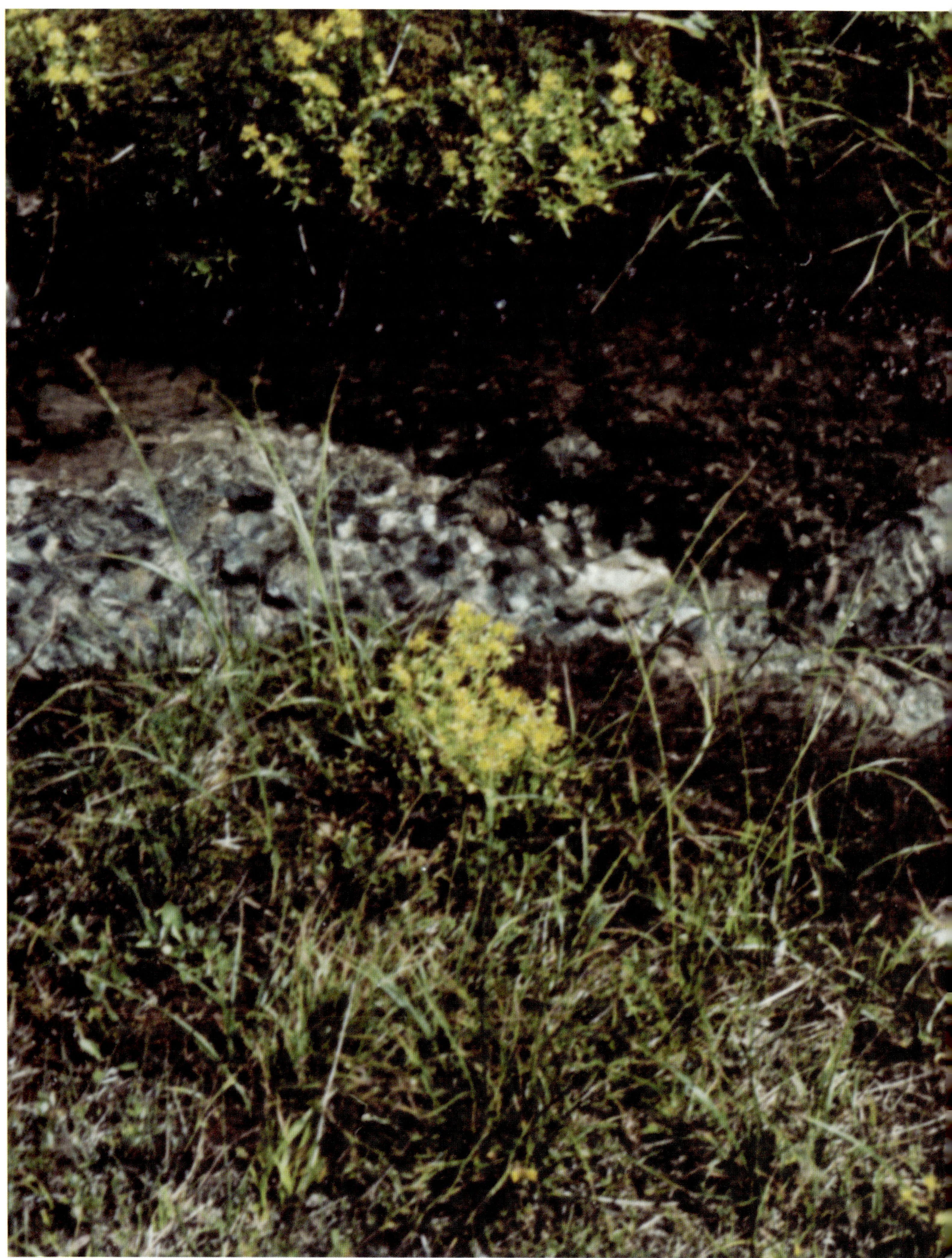

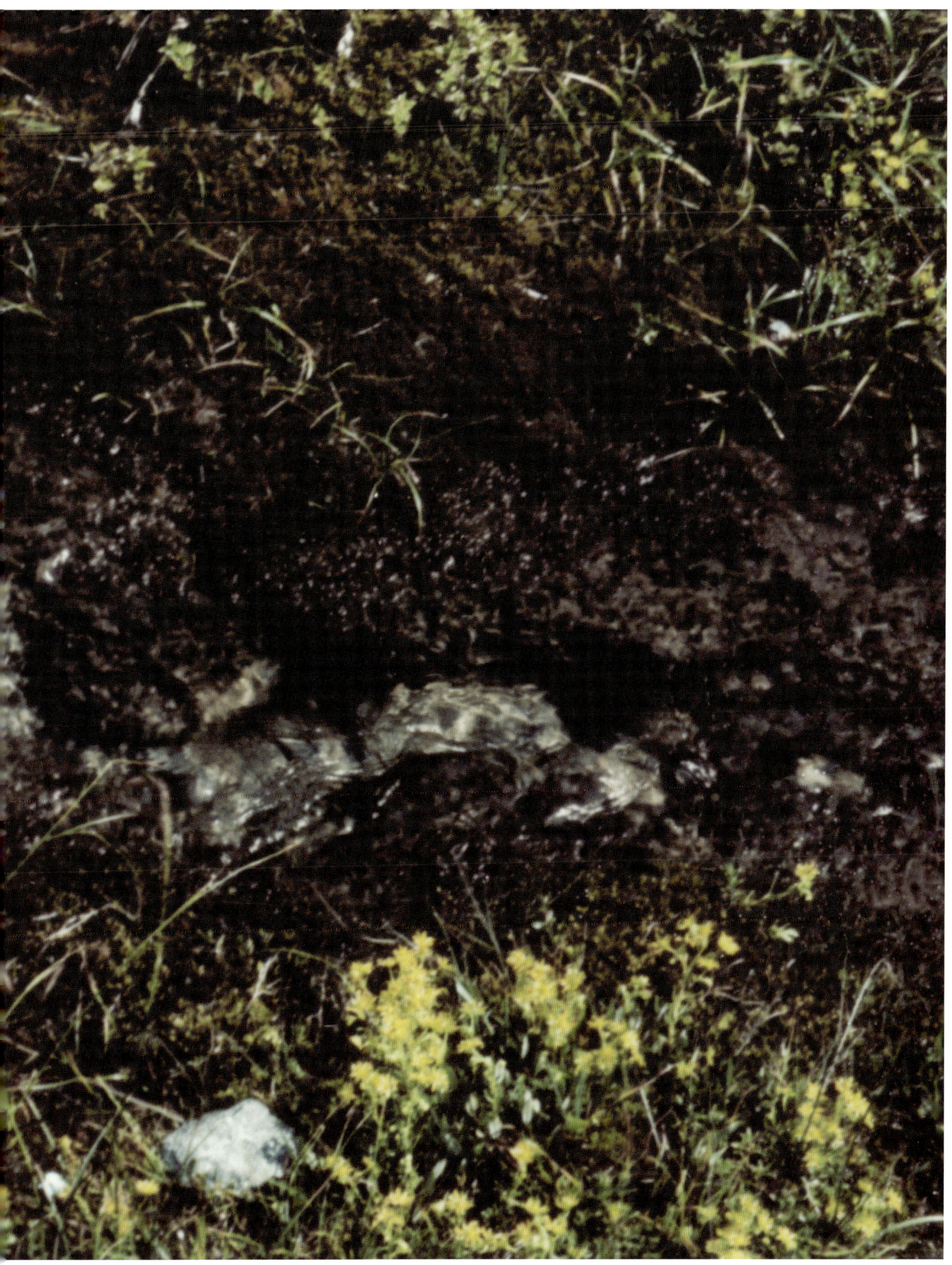

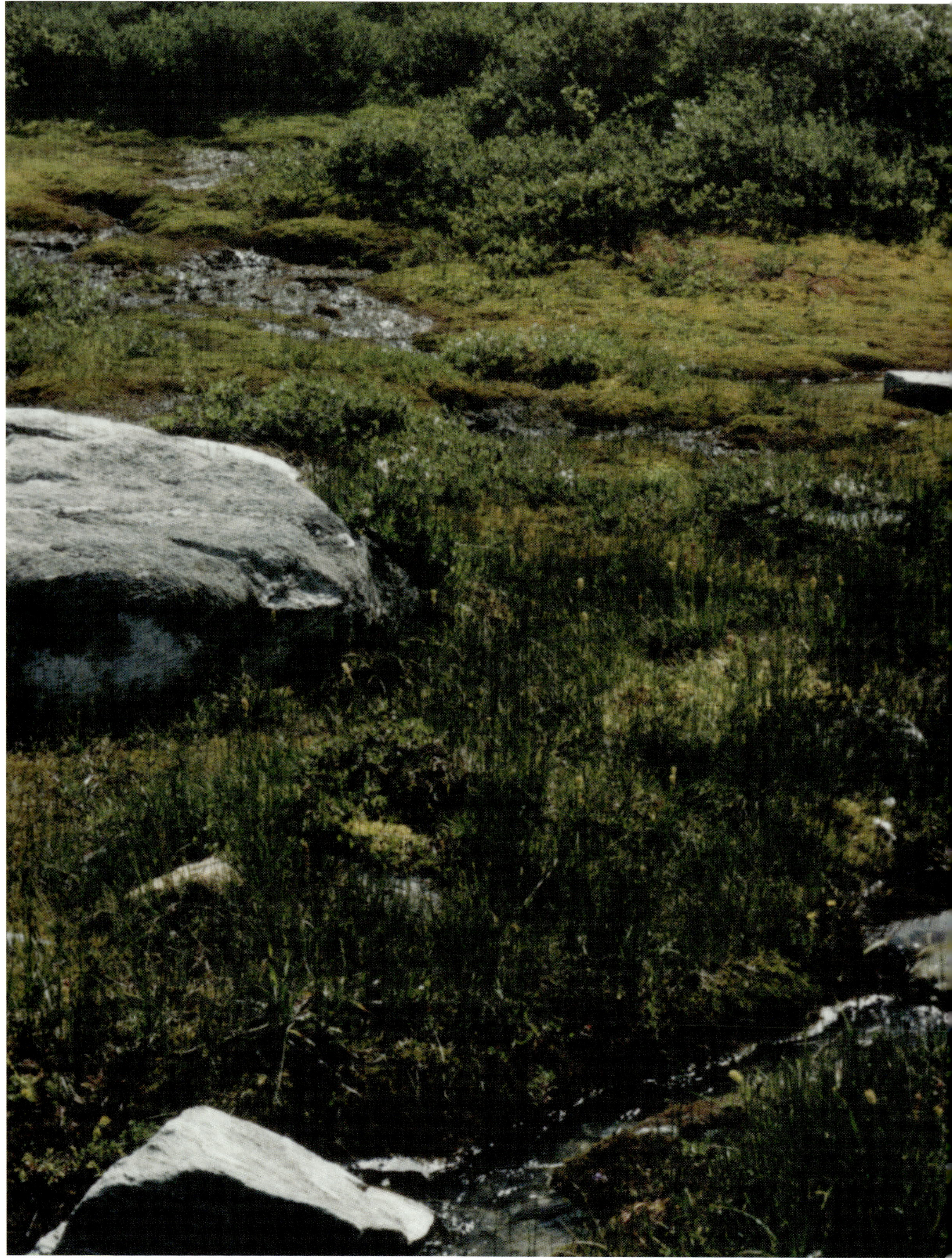

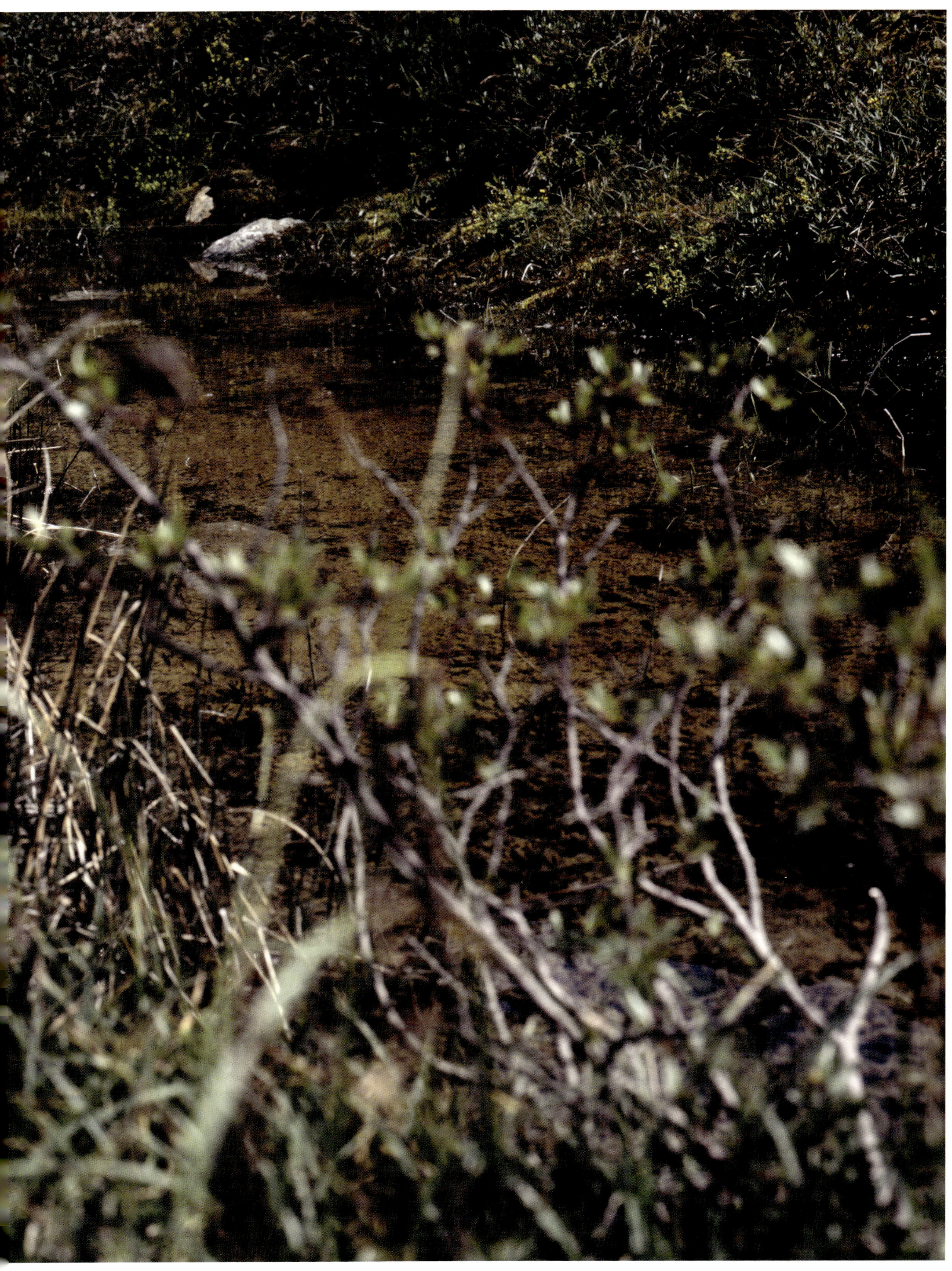

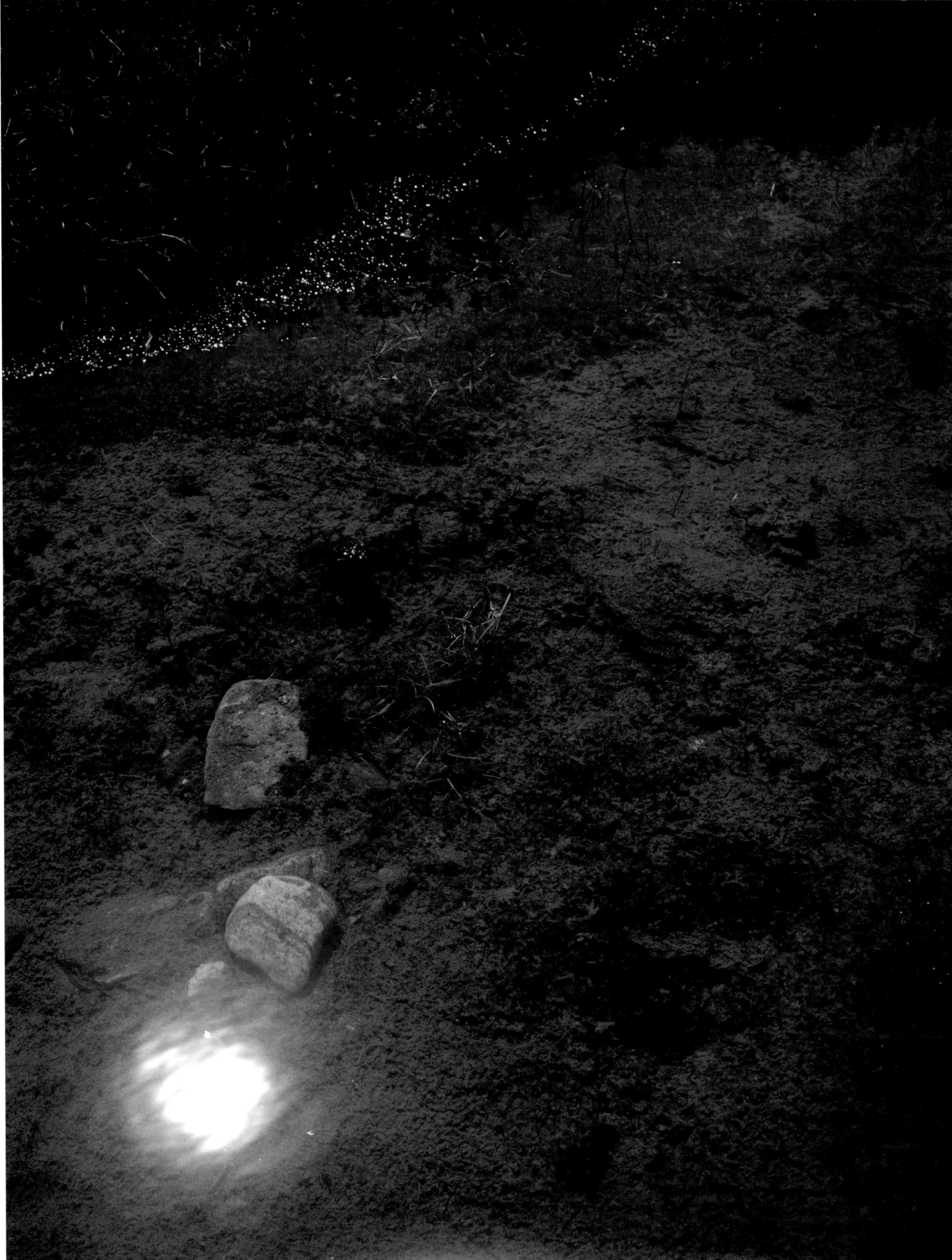

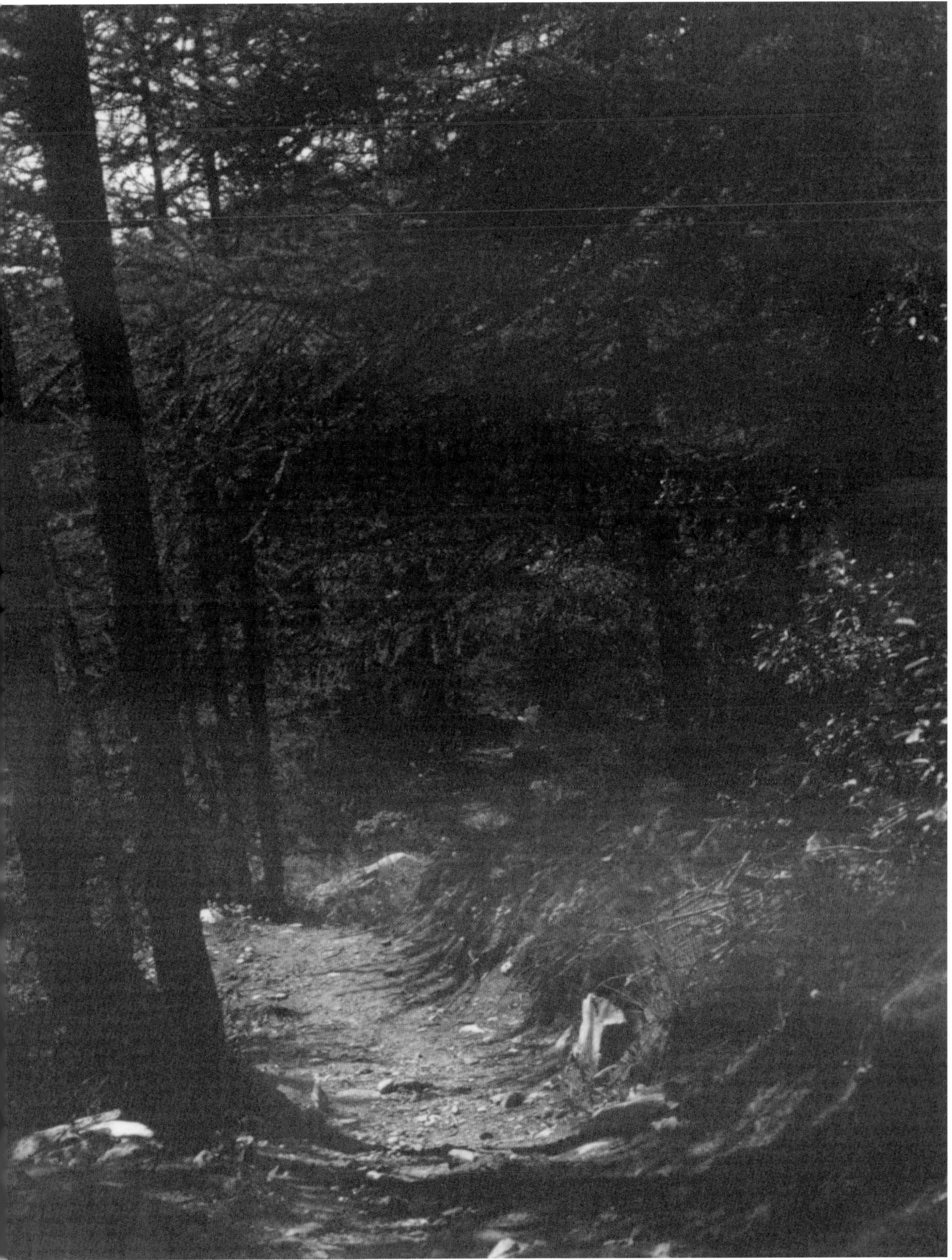

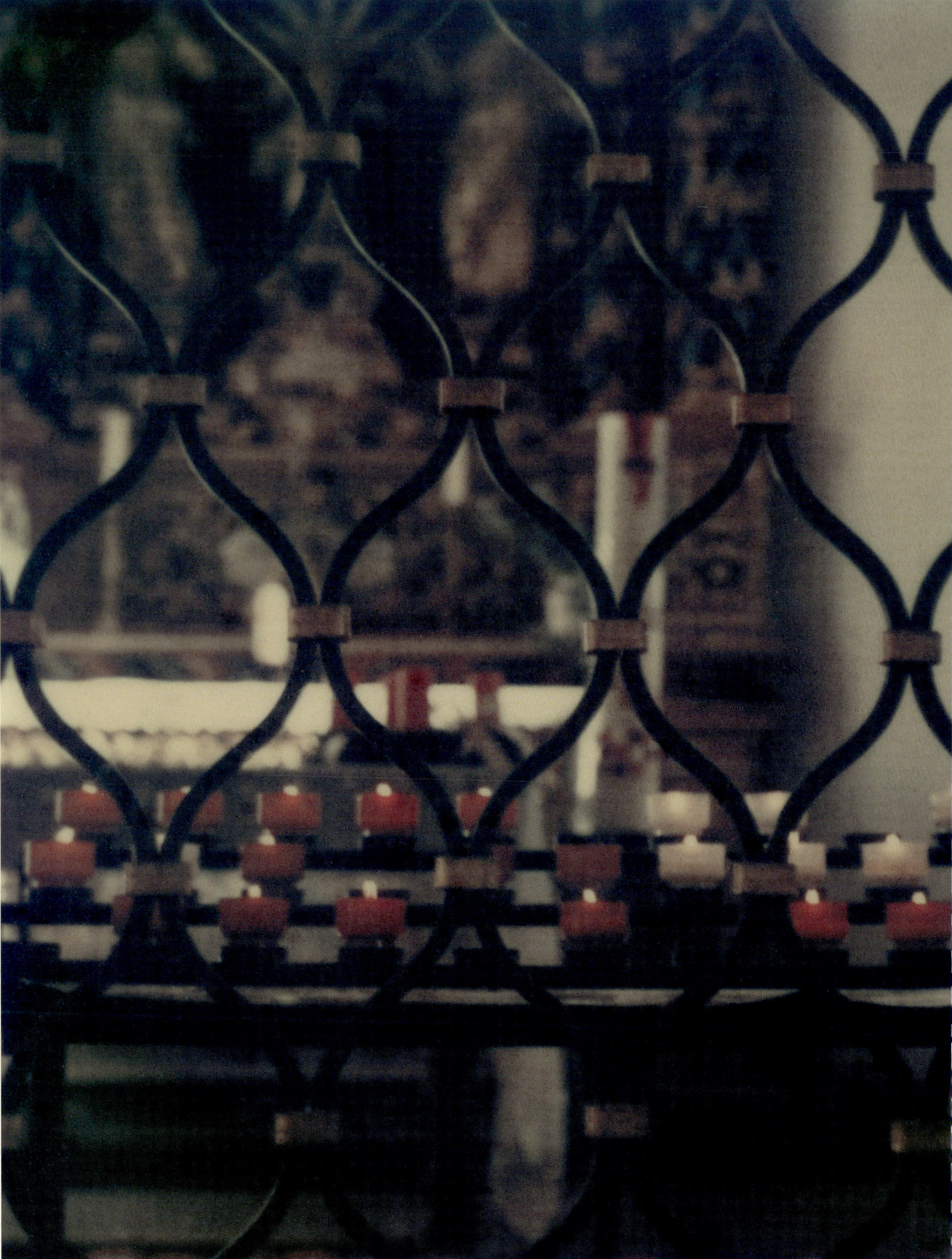

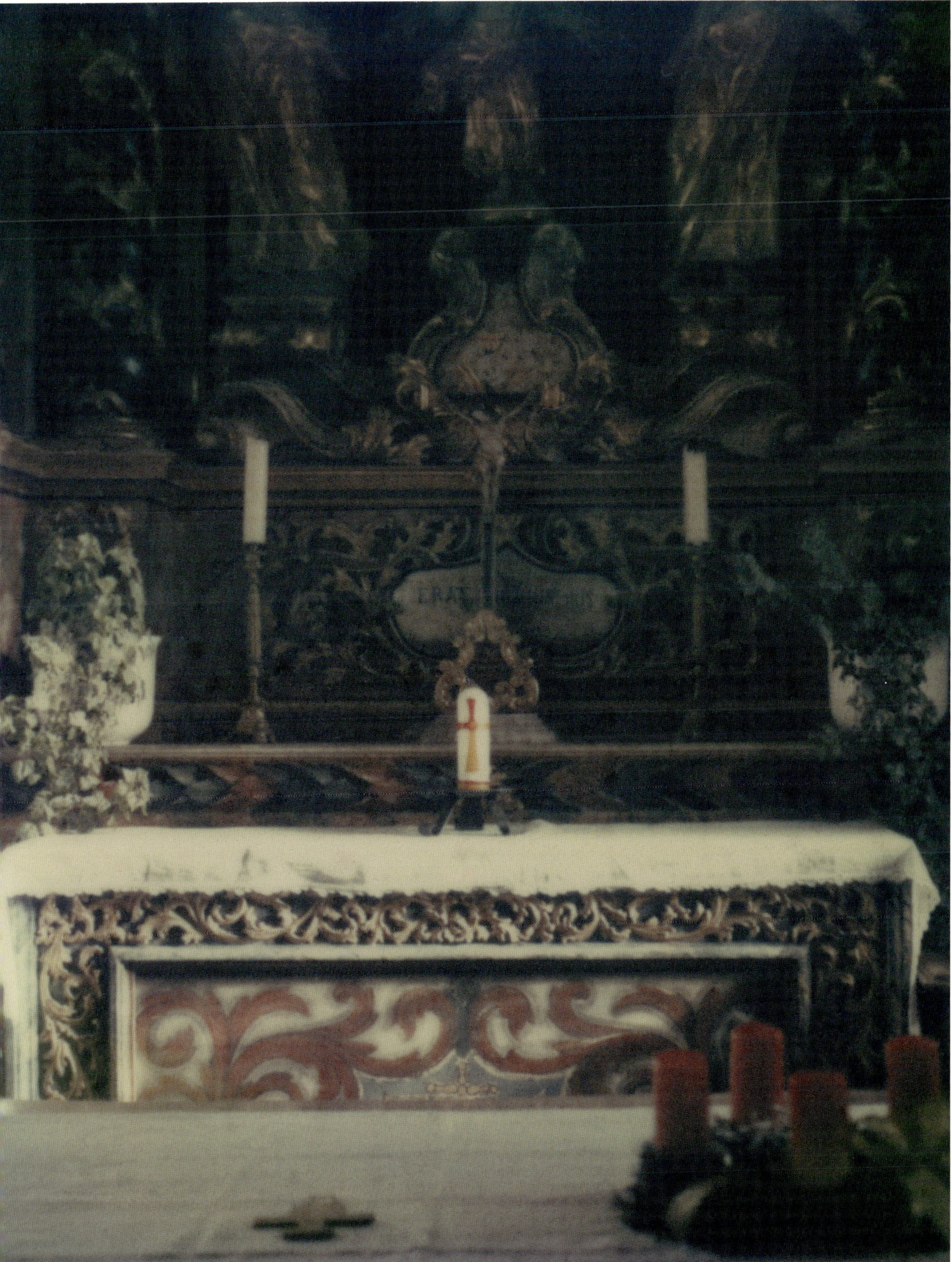

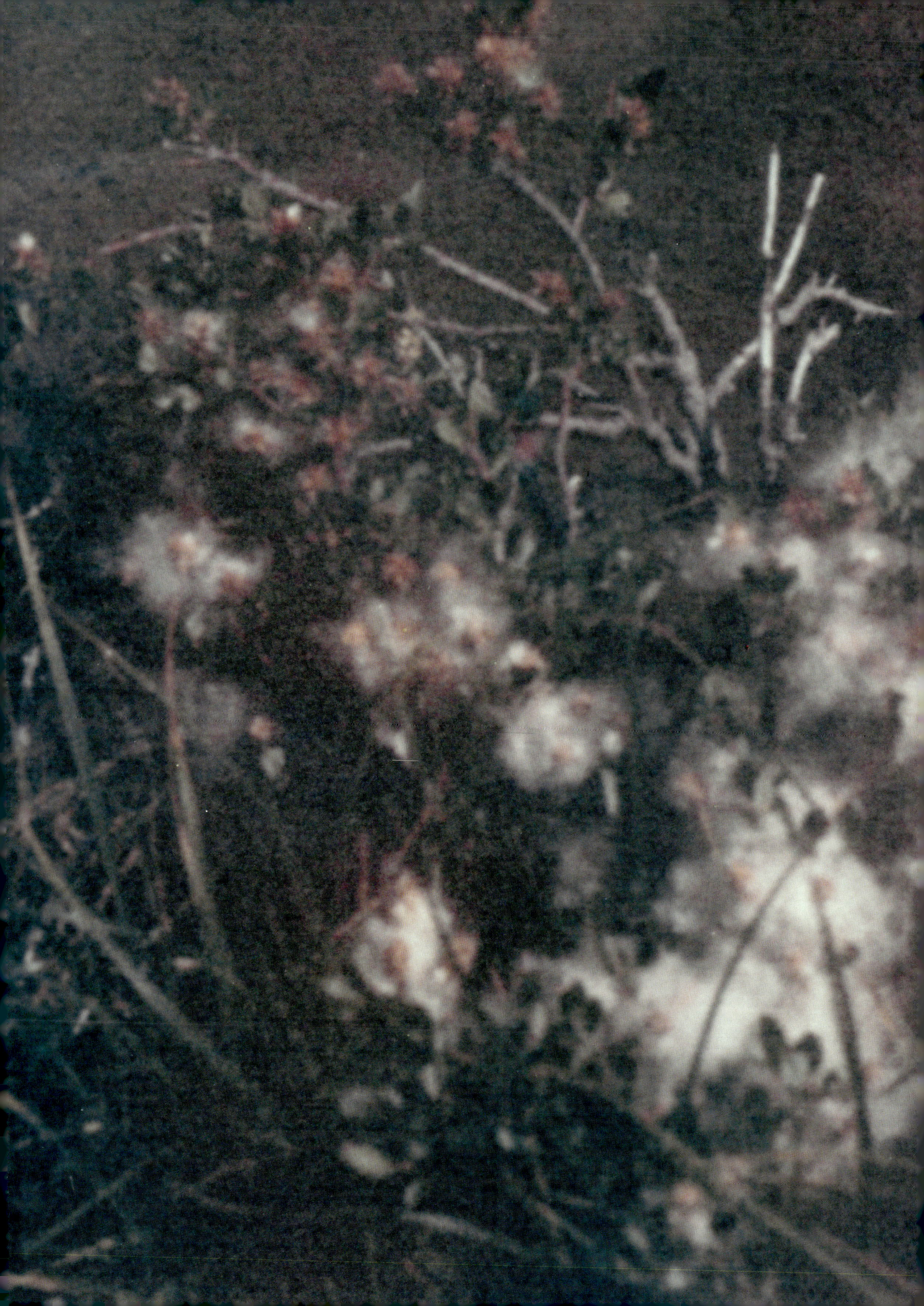

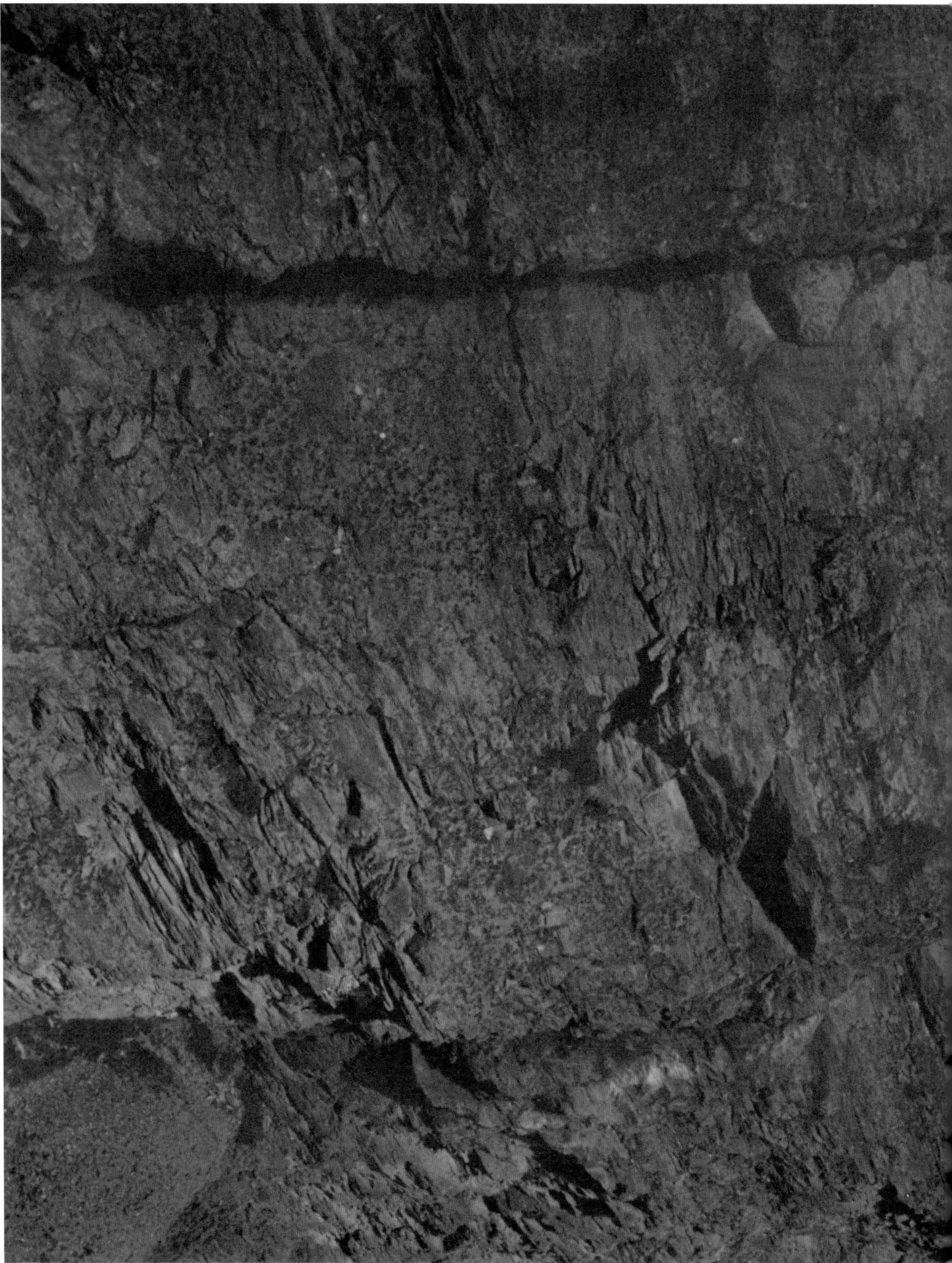

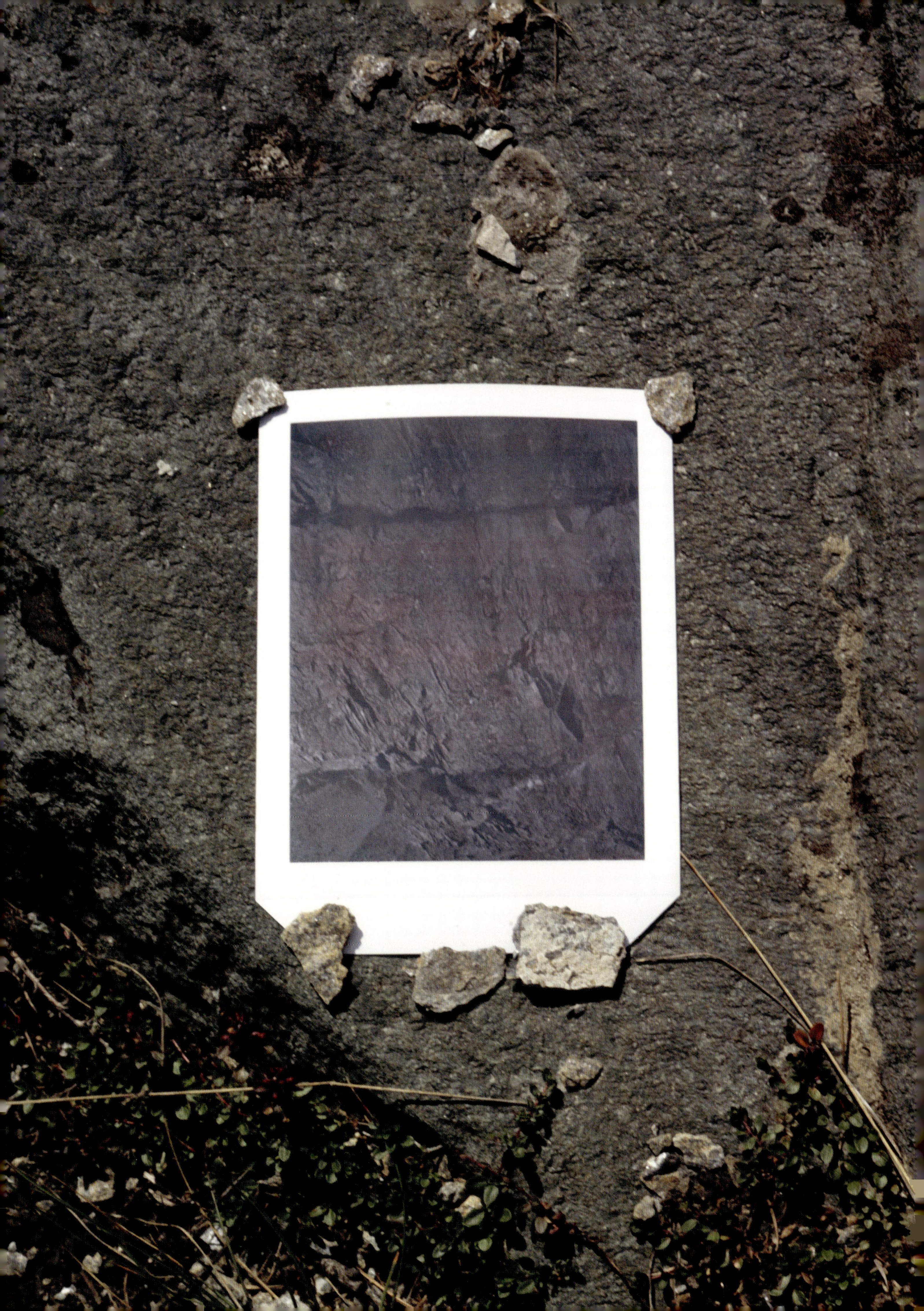

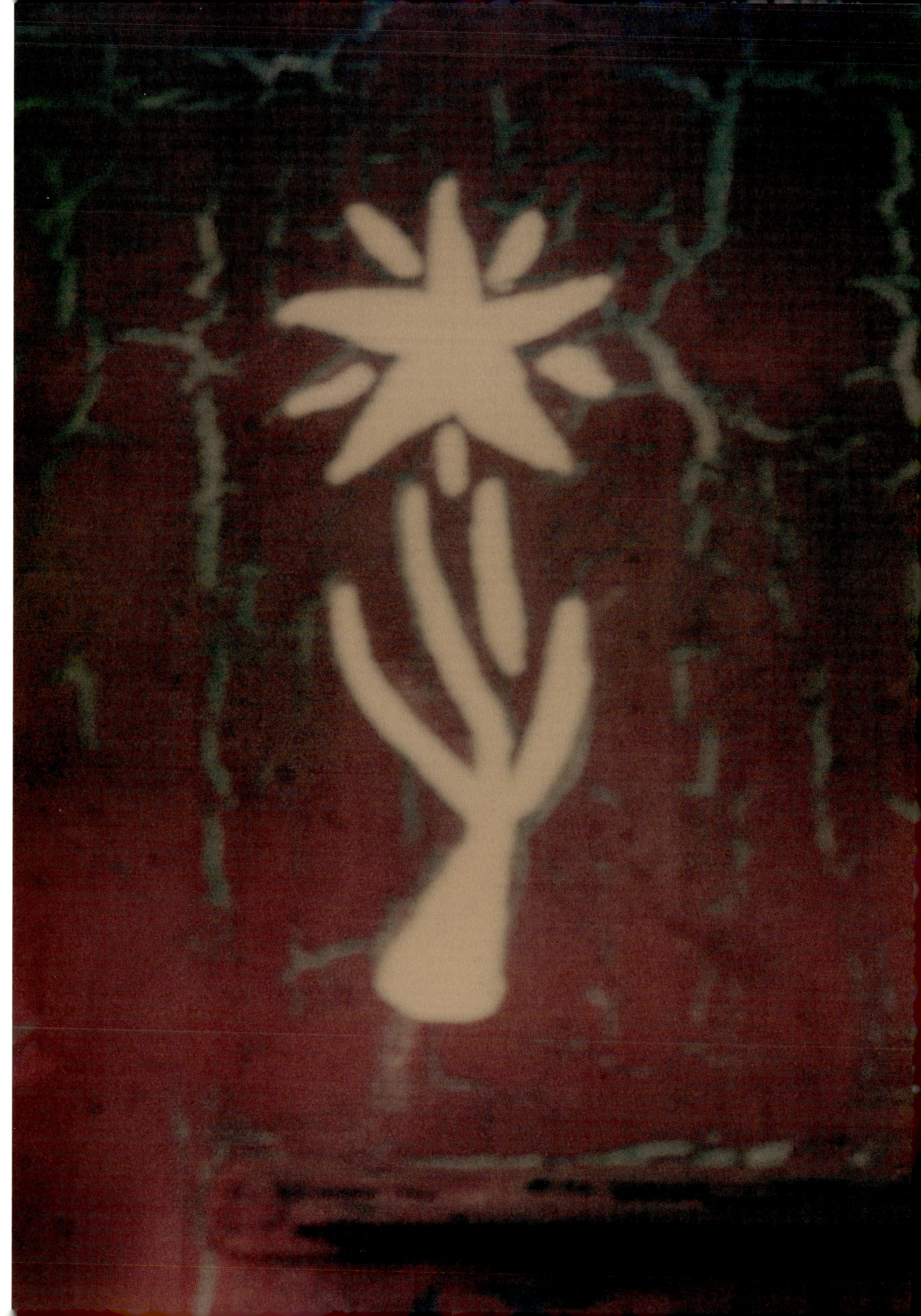

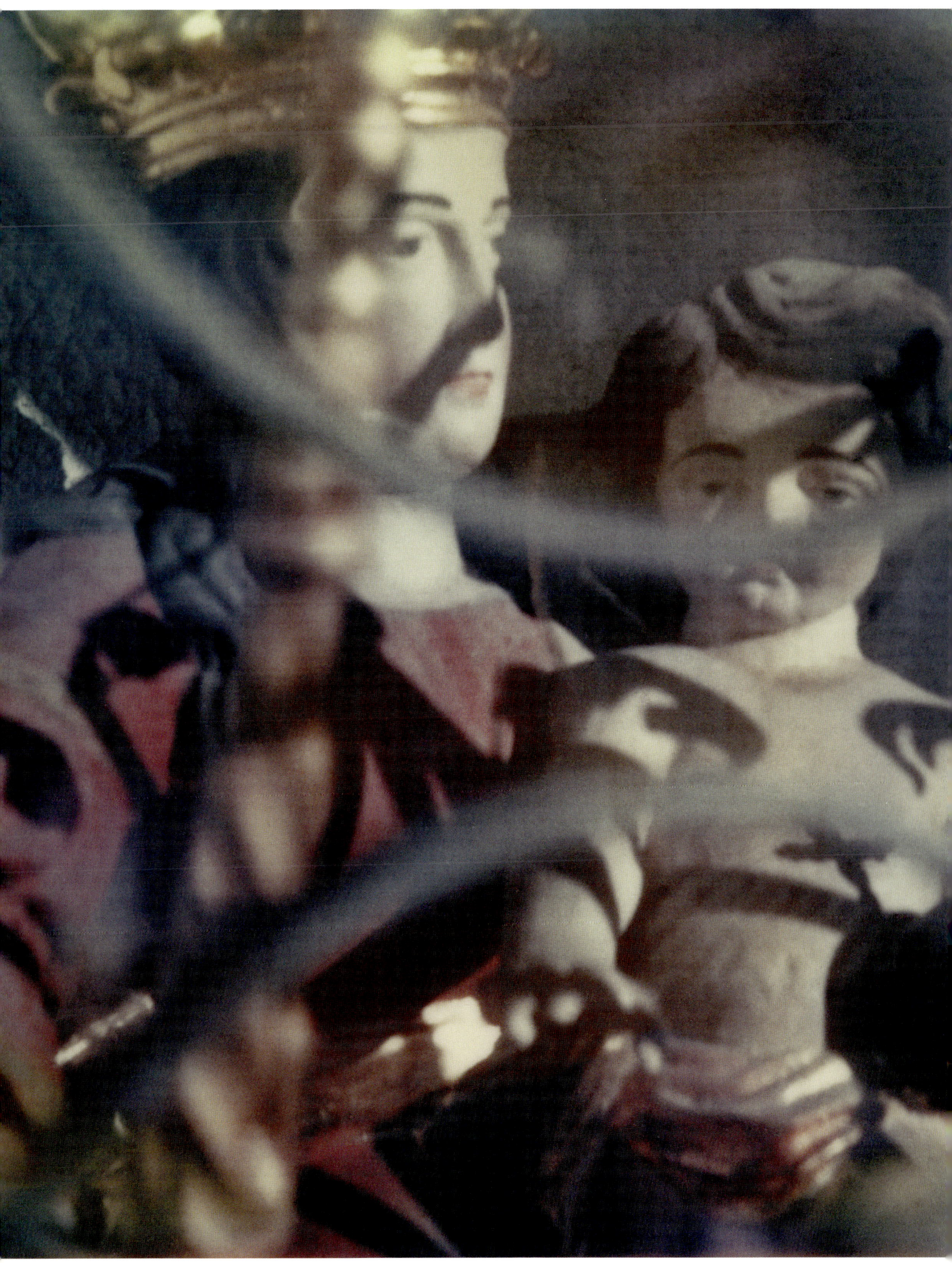

STEIDL
DÜSTERE STR. 4 / 37073 GÖTTINGEN, GERMANY
PHONE +49 551 49 60 60 / FAX +49 551 49 60 649
MAIL@STEIDL.DE
STEIDL.DE

ISBN 978-3-86930-580-6
PRINTED IN GERMANY BY STEIDL

—